Additional Praise for *Taming the Money Sharks*

"For those investors who want to profit from the investment markets like professionals, this book is the key to success in eight simple steps. You will find Professor Cheng's investment language in sync with our daily lives—complex theories are replaced with real-life examples and interactive illustrations pinpoint the fundamental knowledge we all need to know to accumulate and protect our wealth."

—Patrick K.S. Wong, Former General Manager, Jardine Fleming Taiwan Investment Management Ltd; Investment Director, Jardine Fleming Unit Trusts Ltd Hong Kong; President, Polaris Investment Trust, Taiwan

"Mr. Cheng has written a highly readable guide for individual stock market investors who wish to develop an organized approach to creating and managing their portfolios. He uses real-life examples to effectively illustrate investing pitfalls and principles, while presenting tools and techniques that are valuable to the discipline needed for success in this activity. Rooted in common sense and conservative principles, his investing framework will best serve individuals who are willing to make a serious commitment of time and energy to research, trade execution, and ongoing portfolio management activities."

—*Richard Mellon, Retired Financial Manager*

Taming the Money Sharks

Taming the Money Sharks

8 Super-Easy Stock Investment Maxims

Philip Shu-Ying Cheng

WILEY

Published by John Wiley & Sons Singapore Pte. Ltd.
1 Fusionopolis Walk, #07–01, Solaris South Tower, Singapore 138628

Other Wiley Editorial Offices

John Wiley & Sons, 111 River Street, Hoboken, NJ 07030, USA
John Wiley & Sons, The Atrium, Southern Gate, Chichester, West Sussex, P019 8SQ, United Kingdom
John Wiley & Sons (Canada) Ltd., 5353 Dundas Street West, Suite 400, Toronto, Ontario, M9B 6HB, Canada
John Wiley & Sons Australia Ltd., 42 McDougall Street, Milton, Queensland 4064, Australia
Wiley-VCH, Boschstrasse 12, D-69469 Weinheim, Germany

ISBN 978–1–118–55042–7 (Paperback)
ISBN 978–1–118–55045–8 (ePDF)
ISBN 978–1–118–55044–1 (Mobi)
ISBN 978–1–118–55043–4 (ePub)

Typeset in 11/13 pt. BemboStd by MPS Limited, Chennai, India.
Printed in Singapore by COS Printers Pte. Ltd.

10 9 8 7 6 5 4 3 2 1

This book is dedicated to all the individual investors who have lost money in the stock market. Many of them shared their experiences with me and enabled me to define the focus of this book. I urge my readers to maintain the proper frame of mind and to form good investing habits in order to survive and prosper despite the presence of the money sharks.

Contents

Acknowledgments

Many people have contributed to my thinking about this book over the years, and I would like to thank them all.

Particular thanks go to my family, friends, and coworkers, who helped directly with suggestions that contributed to the writing of this book.

Special names that should be included in these acknowledgments include the following: Nick Wallwork, Publisher, John Wiley & Sons Singapore Pte. Ltd. (for his overall guidance and advice); Gemma Rosey, Development Editor (for her creative editing); Senior Production Editor Stefan Skeen (for his innovative copyediting); Jules Yap,

Editorial Executive at Wiley (for her patient efforts and organization); Stuart Leckie (for his specific Preface suggestions); and Stella Lam (for her meticulous preparation of this manuscript).

Preface

Do you want to swim in possibly "shark-infested waters" and still survive? Better yet, do you want to get rich by taming the money sharks?

Congratulations! In this book you will find eight super-easy stock investment maxims that will enable you either to stay away from the sharks or to protect yourself from them. You can even become rich systematically by drastically simplifying your investments.

Most of us want to get rich, but do not have the following:

1. Time (we are already very busy with regular work, family, friends, entertainment, etc.)

2. Experience (our professions are not directly investment related)
3. Focus (we are generally bombarded by misinformation)

During my 40 years of investing, I have played with many types of money sharks. Based on my battlefield experience along with the lessons I have learned from my own friends and coworkers, I have distilled some down-to-earth steps for you to consider and follow. You may already have read good books on investing, but in this book I have set forth eight super easy-to-follow maxims of investment to optimize your results.

I also realize that readers will have neither the time nor the patience to deal with demanding investment terms, which are typically presented in many investment books. To reduce the frustration involved in dealing with investment terms, I have eliminated them as much as possible, while still presenting effective investment advice.

Even though investment strategies are not "one size fits all," I present some proven principles for dealing with ongoing uncertainties. These will help you reduce your losses and maximize your gains.

I realize that each of you has your own objectives, strategies, and hoped-for results. Thus, I encourage you to modify my investment principles to fit your own portfolio and risk levels, whether you want your investment profits to satisfy near-term objectives (e.g., buying a nice car or a new house), or long-term goals (e.g., saving for a college education or retirement).

This book has eight chapters as highlighted in the flowchart that follows. I recommend that you try to follow as many pointers as possible to be successful. According to my historical feedback, many friends have followed just a few of these principles judiciously and have already enjoyed systematic profits from their investments.

Stock Investment Flowchart as Discussed in This Book

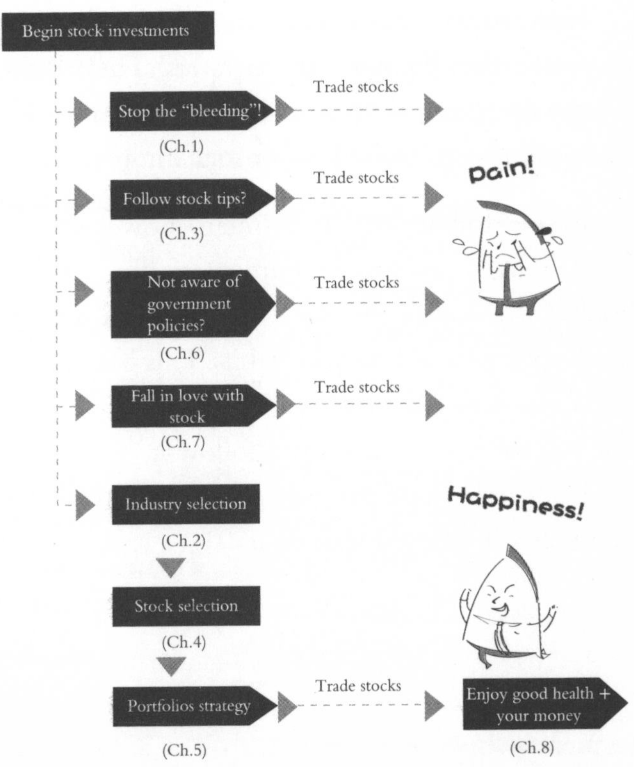

After reading this book, you will be able to "swim in your own investment water" while co-existing with the "money sharks." The sharks referred to in this book are of two types:

A. The first type consists of the huge operators. They execute huge buy–sell orders in the stock market based on their own needs. They do not *purposely* attack individual investors—or any other investors, for that matter. However, because of their huge size, any investor that happens to get in the way of their normal operations would definitely get hurt.
B. The second type consists of malicious sharks who would purposely scheme against any investors (especially individual investors). These sharks use deception to trick and attack unwary investors, causing "blood loss" or total incapacitation.

Please follow my investment flowchart and build a new investment framework for yourself. Follow as many of the eight maxims as possible to form your new investment habits. This book offers not a quick fix but a lifestyle change that will benefit you for many years if you follow it.

I sincerely hope that you profit from this book as much as I enjoyed writing it.

Author's Disclaimer

This book is intended to provide information from sources considered to be reliable, but the author and publisher make no representation or warranty as to their accuracy or completeness, and specifically disclaim any liability, loss, or risk, whether personal, financial, or otherwise, that is incurred as a consequence, directly or indirectly, from the use and/or application of any of the contents of this book.

Chapter 1

Stop the Bleeding

Should You Continue to Invest by Striking While the Iron Is Hot?

Don't chase after any hot asset; first learn why it is hot.

Why do we chase after a hot asset? Please note that a hot asset (or a hot stock) can simply be any asset popularized by the media or any information channels. The story is the same: a newly developed, highly profitable investment opportunity appears, and if the investor does not act immediately, the opportunity will be gone.

This simple answer is just human nature.

We don't want to be dummies and get left behind. Besides, all the "smart people" are already in it. This is a powerful motivation for us to jump in on a hot stock or asset. Often, it is mentally satisfying to join the "winners."

It is always tempting to chase after a hot asset as a result of sheer emotion. None of us wants to be left behind in a hot cycle when a lot of money can be made by simply going with the trend. As the momentum keeps escalating the prices, the quick profits (even on paper) are instantly gratifying.

A. Chasing a Hot Stock

When a hot stock price begins to jump, we may also rationalize that even if we lose money, we are not to be blamed; *we* are simply "unlucky" as a group. That is such a human impulse, yet the fact is that investors still can lose a lot of money, unwisely at that, if they do not truly understand the reasons behind the price increase.

From an industry standpoint, recall the tech boom years of 2000 and 2001. In addition to the basic industry innovation, the flow of funds from all over the world kept pumping up the unrealistic stock prices of the tech companies, way beyond their respective intrinsic values.

Recall also that before the tech bubble burst, many opportunistic companies changed their existing names to an Internet or high-tech name, such as "ABC High Tech Company," or "XYZ Internet Company." Then these companies would announce to the media how their great innovations would work. It was amazing how many investors got sucked in, guided by the "strike while the iron is hot" mentality, even though these companies had little or no expertise in their newly acquired hot products.

After I had just graduated from college with an engineering degree, my first investment was based on just listening to a hot name and going with it. My first administrative assistant, Amy, urged me to buy a stock that Joe (her newly wedded husband) recommended highly as a big winner. Joe had just joined a major brokerage company and was eager to get new clients, and Amy helped him to do some sales pitching and highlighted a "hot" stock to me.

This ABC pharmaceutical company had just tested a new cancer drug that promised to kill cancer cells of virtually all types. Preliminary lab testing indications appeared favorable, yet the final government approval was still pending. Joe highly recommended this "must win" stock to his friends and me, saying we should get in early to enjoy the big price appreciation.

With only $4,000 in my bank account, I was not ready to make a killing. However, both Amy and Joe kept up the pressure, saying that this was the opportunity of my lifetime to get filthy rich. Succumbing to my greed instinct, I put in $2,000, half of my net worth at that time.

Sure enough, the stock went ballistic. Increasing from $10 (my entry price) to $15 in just two weeks, a 50% gain; I was a happy man. I was going to buy more, but at the counseling of my family members, I did not put in any more money. Meanwhile the stock went to $20 after another week. I was angry. "What a dummy," I was saying to myself. How could I be so stupid and so conservative? No guts!

Four weeks went by, and the government finally issued its statements and disapproved the cancer drug. The stock now crashed from $20 to $5. Totally shocked by this news, I was scared and sold the stock by taking a big loss of $1,000. I had lost 25% of my net worth!

Key Point

The moral of this story is that we simply cannot follow a hot tip and invest without understanding the stock.

Following this experience, I had many potential "hot winners" recommended to me, which I mostly declined after doing a little homework. I never can forget this cancer stock incident. In retrospect, the 25% loss of my net worth was an expensive tuition to pay, but it was well worth it. My feeling is that such incidents are not uncommon; many of us may have had a similar experience.

In many countries, pharmaceutical company stock prices also showed large volatility due to various company events, sector environment, and consumer protection factors. This applies not only to the pharmaceutical industry, but to all industries. None of us wants to miss an opportunity to buy a stock before its price explodes. We should also appreciate that the media folks work hard to bring us the breaking news about a company.

Key Point

Unless investors have already done their homework on both the industry and the company, there are better ways to invest their hard-earned money.

We all understand that any company can increase profitability and cash flows as a result of unwise short-term decisions. There are many historical examples of top management's pushing their companies to stratospheric heights of growth and profitability by engaging in unprecedented leveraging activities or through the use of derivatives. As the stock prices went up, all those noncore business activities were ignored by investors and speculators alike. No one seemed to care about those activities as long as the stock prices kept going up.

Key Point

Eventually, it was a case of musical chairs; when the music stopped, many people suffered big losses.

Why and how does a stock become hot? Was it pumped up by an analyst or the media, or by a bogus story, or simply by a rumor? Other than a truly bona fide growth stock situation, a stock can be made "hot" in numerous ways, as discussed further in Chapter 3. Let us just mention a few here:

1. A company determines to push up its price by its own advertising and other promotional campaigns, primarily using its own resources.
2. There is a wide coverage by brokerage firms for a stock that they select to endorse.
3. A stunning story is widely covered by TV, radio, newspapers, and other media regardless of its relative impact on a company.

4. A bogus story is widely circulated at dinners and cocktail parties by "already-in" investors.
5. A "conspiracy story" comes from a large investor who would take profits ahead of retail investors after they are "sucked in" and prices have gone up.

Therefore, let these possible scenarios be warnings. Tread cautiously; it is your own hard-earned money!

B. Chasing a Hot Trend

A hot trend can develop anywhere in the world, usually as a result of some economic or political conditions. Let me cite three examples, one during the early 1600s in Europe, one in the late 1990s in Asia, and one in the United States around 2000. Note the presence of the common speculative mentality that has no basis in fundamental analysis.

1. Tulip Bulb Bubble (Holland)

The tulip was first brought to Holland in the middle of the sixteenth century, and upscale citizens soon collected and treated these tulip bulbs as status symbols, like precious gems. As prices rose, everyone saw the opportunities to speculate and made money in a very short time.

As the momentum gathered speed, prices were rising so fast that dealers were trading in their animals, land, and houses for more tulip bulbs. At the height of this "hot trend," tulip bulbs were trading at such a feverish pace that the prices reportedly increased manyfold in less than a month.

When people realized that the bulbs were overpriced in 1637, panic selling began. Prices crashed to a fraction of acquisition costs, leaving many speculators in financial ruin.

2. Property Market (Hong Kong)

From 1995 to 1997, the Hong Kong property market was hot and gradually developed into a housing bubble. During such a hot cycle, one can always dream up a thousand valid reasons explaining why this hot cycle would continue forever. Two popular reasons were the following:

1. Large immigrant flow from China would continue to push Hong Kong property prices up. After all, 1.3 billion people are in China; think of the potential.
2. China would not let Hong Kong's prosperity peter out after the 1997 handover. Meanwhile, real estate stocks were very hot. Unless one got in and out quickly, one could get badly burned. Alternatively, if one had a deep pocket, then one could stay in the game for a long time and would probably profit accordingly.

3. Dot-Com Bubble (United States)

This historic speculative bubble occurred approximately between 1997 and 2001. Beginning around 1997, new Internet-based companies experienced rapid rises in their stock prices due to a combination of promotion from venture capitalists and sheer speculation by stock investors, among other factors.

As with any hot trends, many investors were willing to overlook traditional financial evaluation tools in favor of blind faith in a "great leap forward," in technological advancements in this case.

The technology-heavy NASDAQ Index peaked at 5,048 in March 2000, representing the crest of the bubble; it should be noted that this doubling of the index record was attained in less than a year. This dramatic increase finally could not be sustained when the bubble broke, causing a loss of approximately $5 trillion in the market value of the companies involved.

Key Point

During any hot asset trends, investors should investigate to determine how real they are and how long they will continue.

C. Maxim No. 1: Don't Rush into Buying, and Avoid Further Bleeding

1. Cool Down

What we need to do is to first cool down and then to determine whether the hot asset will continue to be hot and for how long—that is, to determine the realistic conditions pushing up the prices. Often, there could be true economic conditions that contribute to the successful hot cycle. On the other hand, they may be only temporary imbalances in the supply and demand of certain assets. You should act responsibly.

Key Point

Before investing in the hot asset or any purchase of similar assets, you should have a basic knowledge of the supply and demand of such assets, as explained in Chapter 2.

To be fair, an asset or a stock can become hot because of temporary speculation in the particular asset as well as certain underlying basically sound fundamentals that would then last for quite some time.

For example, as this chapter was being written in mid-2012, many economists predicted that global chronic inflation was coming. Among numerous other policies, central banks around the world were resorting to "quantitative easing" as a major policy for stimulating their respective economies.

Thus, many financial advisors promoted gold as an investment vehicle, because no one can "print more gold." However, investors need to judge their own personal situations and adopt portfolio strategies appropriately. They should not rush in and buy gold simply based on a macro phenomenon.

As discussed in Chapters 4, 5, and 6, investors should invest based on their own risk profile and do appropriate due diligence. For example, using gold as an investment target, some basic questions arise:

- What type of gold to invest in—physical gold, gold mining stocks, gold mutual funds, or gold jewelry?
- When to invest—one lump sum or dollar cost average? Technical charts can help with timing.
- Where to invest—locally or in foreign countries? How to resolve amount, pricing, and other related questions: percentage of gold in the total portfolio, holding for a long time or just for short-term speculation?
- If physical gold is chosen should it be stored locally, or with custodians in London, New York, or Zurich? What are the related pros and cons?

2. Simple Verification

As much as your time allows, I advocate a simple common sense verification of the fundamental conditions of the hot asset if that trend continues to evolve. After verification, invest an appropriate percentage of your investable assets accordingly (see Chapter 5).

You may also wish to set your timing as to how long you wish to keep your position. Target a return on investment percentage for that period of time?

For a stock, a good simple technical chart comparing similar stocks would give you the basis for making a reasonable judgment of the "appropriate value" of the current prices of your targeted stock. For a company stock, I further recommend that you look at the most basic financials of the company (see Chapter 4 for a more detailed discussion). The following questions should be asked:

1. Have the company's sales continued to go up? Are they sustainable and for how long? Are they for any one-time event only?
2. Has the profit margin remained at the existing level, or is it increasing? Is it sustainable, and for how long?
3. Has the earnings per share (EPS) been going up due to the expansion of core business activities? Or are the EPS increases due to one-time extraordinary company activity, such as selling the company's fixed assets (e.g., a building or certain subsidiaries)?

4. Has the company's cash flow per share been growing from core operations, or is it increasing due to additional leveraging of the balance sheet, such as through as bank loans?

Basic financial figures and ratios can easily be obtained from popular financial websites, such as www.yahoo.com/finance and www.google.com/finance, among others (see Chapter 4 for detailed information sources). If these quick checks reveal significant issues, go slow before you plunk down your hard-earned money.

3. More Detailed Verification

If your investment is reasonably large, say more than 2% of your portfolio, I recommend a more detailed verification, as suggested in Chapter 4. I do wish to note that the three major financial statements (income statement, balance sheet, and cash flow statement) have definite interactive relationships with each other, and the following five financial ratios provide keys to understanding a company (see Figure 1.1).

What basic fundamentals should investors know? Among others, I recommend five relevant areas to compare for at least three years—if not for five years—to get a trend, depending on the time you have available and performance volatility.

1. Sales growth (%)
2. Gross profit margin (%)

Figure 1.1 Relationships between Balance Sheet, Income Statement, and Cash Flow Statement

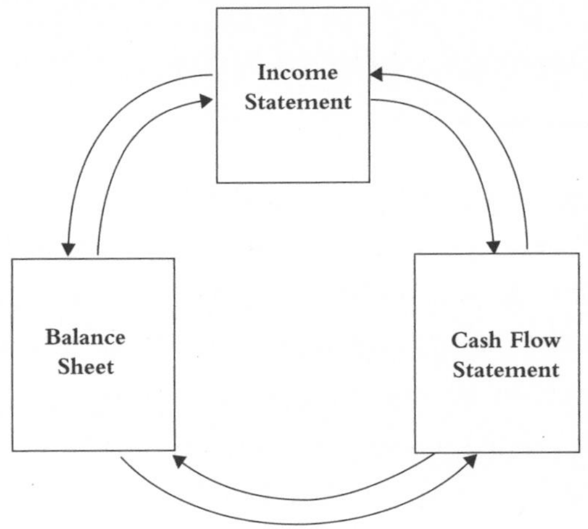

3. Debt-to-equity ratio (%)
4. Net cash flow from core operations ($)
5. Net cash flow from core operations divided by total assets

For a more vigorous financial analysis discussion, see Chapter 4.

For more detailed financial figures, if Google, Yahoo!, or other popular financial websites do not satisfy you, you can always obtain information from the company's websites directly.

Go to their websites and click tabs for "Investor Relations" and then "Financial Information" or similar links—for example, www.IBM.com or www.caterpillar.com—and click on "Investor Relations" and then "Financial Information" and so on. If these trends show abnormalities or issues, you should do a little more homework before you invest.

4. Knowledge of the Industry

I recommend that investors spend time checking out simple stock price charts. Although you don't have to be an expert in reading complicated charts, a simple comparison of similar stocks in the same industry is helpful for getting a feeling. You should be aware of any unusual price movements among similar companies in the same industry.

I also caution investors relying on correlation of statistics, between one industry and another, or one company to another, or one activity to another. Investors should use common sense in interpreting statistics and in judging correlations, if any. Then infer the proper results and make an investment decision accordingly.

For example, to refer to a long-standing joke, the number of new students in the freshman class of a certain U.S. Ivy League university has been recorded as directly correlated with the number of tons of bananas exported by a South Pacific tropical country. We were told that for the past five years, these two numbers were in perfect correlation. Thus can we predict the sixth year now?

As I will discuss in Chapter 2, we should develop certain knowledge of an industry or sector before we invest in a stock in a significant manner.

Action Plan

1. Do not chase after a hot asset without cooling down first. Do study the most basic company information and its historical performance.
2. Do learn and think through the basic financials and fundamentals of an investment as to why it is hot now and how long it may stay hot.
3. Invest only a portion of your investable cash and track regularly as to when to exit with your profit target. Be realistic.
4. When in doubt, observe and wait. Sun Tzu, the great military strategist, observed: "Don't ever start a battle when you feel you may not win! Conserve your resources. Don't fight for the sake of mere action!"
5. Psychologists repeatedly confirm that information alone does not lead to the formation of a habit. Make "stop the bleeding" a habit.

Chapter 2

Select an Industry to Increase Probability of Profitable Investments

Apply Expertise from Work or Personal Interest

Combine investment with work or a personal interest.

A. Basic Knowledge

Stay with one industry or only a few. Don't just invest without any basic knowledge of an industry or sector. If you already have some basic knowledge and then take advantage of your expertise and related business trends, you will make money much more readily.

Investment is unlike shopping. Shopping for variety is fun, but for investment activity, focus is needed, which then leads to profits. That's when fun comes automatically.

At this point, you might feel that my suggestion to invest in one or two industries would totally violate the most basic investment principle: investment risk diversification.

In response I'd say it depends on your investor profile. If you have all the superior conditions, including

- A lot of time
- A lot of energy
- Ample investment funds
- Superior financial analytic skills

then, by all means, if you wish to invest in 10 or 20 industries to spread the risk, go ahead.

However, given that most individual investors do not have the resources of large institutions, they should "conquer" one industry at a time. After you feel knowledgeable about one industry, then certainly you may add another industry for diversification.

To test whether you are ready to invest in an industry as an "expert," you may wish to "paper trade" first—that is, simulate buy–sell orders on your own paper only. After you have gained confidence, then make real-time investments.

Key Point

Based on my years of investment observation of my friends, 8 out of 10 of them would buy stocks in X industry when it gets media attention. By that time, that stock may already be overpriced.

In any case, after a certain number of days if a stock in *Y* industry gets hot, my friends would now buy in, again often at already inflated prices.

This phenomenon would go on, month after month, year after year; my friends would now have stocks in totally different unrelated industries! (*Note*: As a former chief investment officer [CIO] of a large financial institution, I am aware of the large number of worldwide industries. To track these 68 industries and sub-industries, large financial institutions can afford to hire teams of analysts, something simply out of reach for most individual investors.)

One might argue that my friends are doing the right thing. They are simply following the traditional investment rule of diversification. My advice is yes, diversification done the right way is good, but if it's done the wrong way, the original intended diversification benefits still may be illusive.

Most of my friends, who are not reading this book, accumulated 20 to 40 stocks (or more) over the years over many unrelated industries, mostly at inflated prices, as they do not have time to learn and judge the buy-in price levels appropriately. For them, the original diversification intention is noble and correct. But they have not "known thyself" as to why this intention has been disastrous for them. They simply do not have the time and knowledge to track these industries.

Key Point

What is the result of blind and mindless diversification? Diversification of a sheer large number of stocks often leads to diversification of losses, not diversification of risk.

By concentrating on one industry at a time, you would soon learn how a business cycle affects that industry. Based on the nature of a boom or recession, certain industries will be affected more. The more you track the historical relationships, the better you are prepared to formulate your future buy–sell strategies.

It is beneficial for an investor to note how good and bad times affect an industry, such as

- Basic supply and demand of the business's products and/or services
- How a stronger competitor can keep sales growth intact
- How certain companies can maintain their competitive advantages and thus their profit margins
- How net positive cash flow can continue to be generated by means of specific business strategies

By learning how business cycles affect a certain industry, you will be able to see the vulnerability of an industry. Thus my advice is to learn one industry at a time; if you deem it to be superior, stick with it and buy the best companies in that industry.

How would you start evaluating a business or industry? Without becoming overly financial mathematically at this juncture, as will be covered in Chapter 4, the following criteria are basic:

- You should be able to understand the industry's basic demand of products and/or services—for example, how demographic changes would affect sales.
- Closely related to the preceding factor, how do the companies make profits; what are the major costs, capital expenditures, worker wages, overheads, and expense components?
- How much do profits turn to real cash flows, so they are actually available for buying new equipment or new subsidiaries?
- From an owner's standpoint, is the return on invested capital growing or declining?

Note that these are common sense questions. If you can be comfortable with your answers regarding your target industries, you should consider them viable and continue your homework.

But how would you start to pick an industry? Let me suggest two basic approaches, in addition to others that cause you to believe that you have a competitive judgment edge based on your own personal profile.

B. Choosing an Industry to Invest In

I can make the choice easy for you in two ways.

1. Start with Your Own Work

The first easy way to know an industry is to start with your own work or profession.

Many of you are professionals in specialized industries, but may not be in finance or investments. For example, John was the head of an IT department in a multibillion-dollar asset insurance company. John is very smart and very knowledgeable in the IT field, given his 25 years in the industry. However, he confided to me that his stocks had always been losing money.

He told me he had been trying to take advantage of every profitable stock situation deemed to be attractive at that time. The results, however, had been miserable.

I advised him to stick with buying investments only in the IT industry. Just stick with this for one year, I urged, and he agreed. (*Note*: Since John was working full time, one year was appropriate for him. For readers who can devote themselves full time to investment activities, 90 days may be adequate, depending on the complexity of the industry.)

John trusted me and made a promise to me, as an experiment. He began to study all the major IT-related companies in the global arena. His homework included basic fundamental and financial analysis of the target companies with respect to IT industry trends and markets. He started to look into Google, Apple, Cisco, and similar organizations.

In my years of banking and investments, I was forced to learn that in every industry, the financial statements have their own characteristics. It thus follows that each industry has its own norm (or at least an acceptable range) of financial ratios. For example, take the gross profit margin ratio of a typical IT products manufacturing company.

Given the nature of an IT products company, comparatively speaking, the costs of sales are much less than that of, say, a grocery chain-store company, thus allowing for higher gross profit margins. For the IT products industry, the gross margin (FY 2011) was approximately 44%. This is in contrast to the grocery chain industry with an average of approximately 23%.

So if an investor is not aware of the typical range of the gross profit margin of an industry, it would be meaningless (or at least not helpful) in evaluating a target company's financial health against its respective industry peers.

John was buying Apple stocks (AAPL) beginning in 2008 and through 2010 with costs averaging below $200 per share. As of early 2013, the price was approximately $450 per share, which is a fairly handsome profit.

I might add that John did not become afraid when AAPL prices dropped below $100 in early 2009. Instead of panicking like other investors, John just bought more via different tranches, as he was confident and knew the intrinsic value of such a good company.

In Chapter 4, I highlight five key financial indicators and would encourage you to evaluate your target company against other companies in the same industry.

As a result, after doing exhaustive homework, in addition to AAPL (see Figure 2.1) he also bought into Google at the right time, along with other stock purchases. I must emphasize that even for very good companies like these, marketing and financial conditions may be better or worse due to global changes, and investors must continue to track their investments and take appropriate actions when warranted.

In other words, even for great companies, as mentioned, their stock prices will fluctuate based on the "perception of buyers and sellers at any one time"!

Meanwhile, temptations continued from other industries in the form of "strong buys" from John's usual sources, stock gurus from TV programs, analysts from brokerage houses, stock columnists from newspapers, and so on. But John stuck to his guns, unwaveringly. John kept his promise to me.

Since John knew the IT trends of these businesses, including software, hardware, and all the related business models, he was suddenly making money, to his total surprise. He knew when to get into a stock and when to get out. He was a happy IT guy.

Any investor must recognize that for every company, there are easily dozens of key financial figures and indicators. Until and unless an investor concentrates on one particular industry, those key financial figures and indicators would not contribute to a critical assessment of financial conditions.

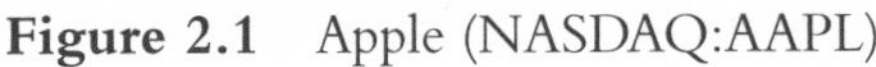

Figure 2.1 Apple (NASDAQ:AAPL)

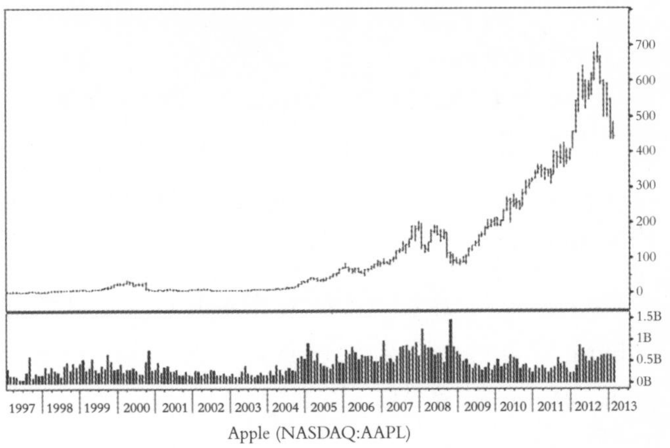

Source: Chart courtesy of HKET Ltd.

Key Point

Generally speaking, the behavior of the financial indicators is characteristic of that industry only. Thus, lessons from financial analysis can be learned and made useful when comparing similar companies in the same industry primarily.

Most chief investment officers (CIOs) of large institutions can easily concentrate on 10 to 20 (or more) industries. They can be successful tracking the financial ratios of chosen industries because

1. The CIO and his team of analysts are working full time.

2. These analysts are professionally trained and have MBA, CFA, CPA, or other degrees or certifications.
3. They have access to powerful computer hardware and numerous high-priced software models to access and analyze tons of data in literally minutes.

Now you can begin to realize how "weak" an individual investor is compared with an institutions' resources.

Key Point

If an average individual cannot compete on 68 industries or sectors, that individual may still excel in one or very few industries and still have a fighting chance.

For example, to determine a company's total value (or its stock value, after being divided by number of shares), there could be easily 10 or more methodologies. The more common ones include

- Book value, which could be approximated by net worth divided by number of shares
- Asset liquidation value, using net assets after accounting for shrinkages and the like: asset liquidation value divided by number of shares

- Asset replacement cost (more appropriate for certain industries): replacement cost divided by number of shares
- Dividend discount value: discounting the value of future dividends (or any forms of positive cash flows) divided by number of shares

Many computer programs are available from large institutions to calculate the foregoing values and thus approximate how a stock should be valued, making the calculation in minutes.

An average small investor simply does not have these resources, not to mention the time and skill needed to analyze the computer outputs, even after the results have been calculated. Therefore, one must focus on just one or a very few industries to acquire expertise on their respective valuation methodologies.

As discussed in Chapter 4, basic industry valuation of companies is critical in setting buy–sell order prices of chosen companies.

2. Own Personal Interest

The second easy way to know an industry is to start with your own hobby or personal interest, as shown in the following example.

a. Mary, the accountant Let us consider Mary who has been an accountant for a number of years.

Her investment results had been disastrous, because she had been hopping from company to company depending on the prevailing fad. When I advised her to stay in accounting-related stocks, she declined. She said she wanted to get away from financial numbers for a change of mood during non-working hours. For that I don't blame her.

When I began to ask for her hobbies or personal interests, she simply said none. I respected her honesty. I started to grill her for anything that she might like but came up blank. Finally, after I questioned her some more, she admitted that she had only one pastime: shopping.

Then I recommended to her that even shopping could be an investment industry homework target if she put her mind to it. Many companies within the consumer industries can be good investment targets if you know them well. Mary was delighted.

I also found out later that Mary loves to shop at Tiffany, Coach, LVMH, Prada, and other luxury consumer goods companies. She loved handbags and jewelry, and other such things. I began to counsel her that she should study the financial backgrounds of these companies and learn their business models, finding out how Tiffany, Coach, LVMH, or Prada could be so successful. I encouraged her to do basic fundamental analysis and some simple tracking of their stock prices and how they correlate with certain economic cycles and consumer sentiments.

Again, I made her to promise me, just for one year, not to invest in any stocks outside the luxury goods industry. She agreed. (*Note*: If Mary could have attended full time to this personal investment project, I would have recommended 90 days or 180 days, again depending on complexity of the chosen industry, but Mary was working full time.)

Mary now had a focus as to the due diligence she needed to do in an industry she already knew quite well from the product standpoint. She enjoyed doing her market research, visiting various luxury goods companies and trying to note the strengths and weaknesses of the various companies regarding products, services, fashion trends, and reliability. Her sharp instincts also assisted her in her evaluation of high-class luxury items, from elegant design of jewelries to expert stitching of handbags. She learned by asking pointed questions, whether she was doing her field trips or performing fundamental financial analysis.

She would continue to examine industry and company reports. She would confirm or dispute their conclusions with her newly acquired expertise. Even though she had a full-time job, she began to know why certain companies continued to do well while others just faded away.

Meanwhile, Mary diligently tracked famous luxury goods companies, like a lion stalking a herd of zebras in the African Serengeti. She would set up indicative price levels of sample companies to buy in and get out, with confidence. She was on top of industry trends and consumer spending capabilities. She was able to capitalize on market signals when they appeared, whereas average investors would have missed them totally.

For example, when Tiffany (TIF) stock was selling around \$40 during most of 2007, Mary thought TIF was a superior stock; she waited patiently and stayed in cash. When the TIF price dropped to around \$20 per share in early 2009, due to the 2008–2009 global financial crisis and other factors, Mary decided to buy in via three tranches over six months, thus achieving an average cost of \$23 per share.

When TIF rebounded in 2010 and 2011, Mary thought it appropriate to close out her positions and exited with an average price of $65 per share, a handsome profit indeed!

For the ensuing years, Mary continued to profit from investing in luxury goods companies at the right prices at the right time, such as Tiffany, Coach, LVMH, Prada, and others. In short, the results were very favorable, in terms of both her own pastime and her investments, which made for a happy accountant.

Mary was enjoying the financial results of her homework and became really excited. She informed me that although she generally disliked reading company annual reports, reading the attractive annual reports of luxury goods companies was fun.

b. David, administration supervisor Another case in point was David, who was a supervisor at the administration support department of an engineering company. Like many friends, he bought stocks year after year and lost money year after year. He hopped from one industry to another, depending on what he heard or saw on a particular day, but he never accumulated knowledge about any one single industry.

Like many of my workaholic friends, David did not develop any hobbies or expertise in any industry. Again, after my questioning him for quite some time, I finally discovered that he enjoyed sports whenever he could find time, literally any sports—soccer, basketball, baseball, and others.

As with my previous success stories, I urged David to concentrate on one and only one industry, in this case, the sporting goods industry. I also made David promise me that at least for six months, if not a year, regardless of how other stocks outside his chosen industry appeared to be "big win," he would not stray away from his chosen industry and buy anything else. Reluctantly, David complied.

Given that David is a typical extrovert, concentrating on just one industry was difficult, as he "enjoyed the free styling" in hopping from industry to industry, stock to stock. However, knowing my past track record, he reluctantly agreed.

After his "promise day," David judiciously studied sporting goods companies, both in his own country and around the world. He began to learn how and why sporting products sell well.

Sporting goods companies' marketing strategies were also analyzed and compared. Details of products were dissected to determine why one company sold better than another—for example, why certain shoes were more bouncy, why certain sports shirts were more "breathable," and why certain clothing styles capture new consumer markets. David enjoyed doing his homework as he developed his stock expertise.

David started to study major companies such as Nike, Adidas, Puma, and other famous companies. Systematically, he evaluated and recorded the industry trends, market changes, product quality, and consumer behavior as well as how the major companies captured related opportunities. Using simple financial analysis, as discussed in this book, he verified the relative success of the major companies and prepared for investments.

Before deciding on a company, David compared key financial indicators such as gross profit margin, debt/equity ratio, and so on, against the industry average and among themselves. (For a discussion of the five key financial indicators, see Chapter 4.)

After six months, David gradually began to buy various sporting goods companies' stocks, at the right prices and at the right time. He invested via different tranches, especially when those stock prices dropped below respective intrinsic values.

David was able to make good money repeatedly on just a few stocks in a span of three to four years, fully understanding the nature of the company, its stock prices, its cycles within the overall stock market, and so forth. David was getting good results consistently.

He confided to me later that he was not even "buying at the lowest prices and selling at the highest prices," as many stock gurus claim they can do. David was just an ordinary small investor with no finance degrees, no MBA, and no CFA. Yet he made profits, year after year, systematically. In which stocks? Guess; just one industry, sporting goods only.

Months later, David confirmed to me his success stories. When he felt a target sporting goods company had begun to deteriorate in terms of its products (as confirmed by financial indicators), David decisively switched to another company that had better potential.

He capitalized on his cumulative knowledge of the sporting goods industry, from product innovation to marketing to distribution, while constantly using key financial indicators to confirm his assessment. Since David knew this industry, if the stock prices were overvalued, he patiently waited—in cash. He waited and waited and waited some more until the prices were right; then he bought and profited again. He was a happy supervisor.

Key Point

Do not forget: Often the best action is inaction.

Naturally, you should apply your common sense to judge an industry or sector if the trend is promising. If not, you should switch to another after proper assessments.

As you pick an industry to research, before you decide that this industry has growth aspects you should read as much as you can about the industry; this is the primary research stage. You may start by asking the basic questions about the goods or services in the industry and determining the major risks and opportunities facing the industry.

Certainly, your reading of books, newspapers, magazines, and related websites will give you plenty of basic information. But that's not enough; at some point, you need to stop reading. Instead, you should start verifying what you have read by actually spending time experiencing the real world of your chosen industry, making a reality check.

For example, refer back to our example of John, who picked the high-tech computer industry. In this case, although John does deal with IBM computers and related Microsoft technology as part of his work and career, he would need to confirm specific high-tech products and services, if he were to decide to buy stocks in Apple.

Naturally, John's basic technological knowledge gives him an edge over other investors in understanding the industry. However, if John should decide to invest in Apple stocks, he must do more; he must physically visit retail Apple stores, compare product prices with Apple's competition, talk to Apple computer users, and more to reconfirm what he learned from his primary research.

Referencing another previous example in this chapter, Mary (the accountant) might wish to confirm her primary research by visiting various luxury goods retailers in shopping malls. She might wish to poll the sales clerks of various stores such as LVMH, Prada, Tiffany, and Gucci as to why customers are insisting on particular brands, despite high prices. The answers could vary greatly, possibly involving style, durability, and superior after-sales service. These personal market surveys may or may not match her primary research, and that's precisely their value.

With any reality check, your primary goal is either to confirm your knowledge from primary research or to dispute it. Through the repeated cycles of confirmation between primary research and reality checks, you would soon become knowledgeable enough to evaluate the industry and its major players. This would set the stage for eventually picking the right company stocks to buy, as is further discussed in Chapter 4.

On the other hand, your reality check may shock you if it shows that your earlier primary research of the industry was inaccurate or misleading; then you may need to be realistic and move on to another target industry. For example, numerous industries have recently declined:

- Wired consumer communication hardware is being slowly replaced by wireless and mobile devices.
- The video and records rental business is being slowly replaced by online Internet access.
- Camera physical films manufacturing for consumers is gradually being replaced by digital cameras.

C. Industry Characteristics

Try to think of each industry as having its own "behavior," like a person. One of the major benefits of studying one industry at a time is that you will learn the financial ratios reflecting the nature of the business operations of that particular industry.

For example, an equipment manufacturing business is likely to carry more long-term debt to finance its land, plant, machinery, and equipment. Conversely, a retail brokerage business would have lower debt financing, and if it had any, it would probably be shorter term.

To facilitate the business financial analysis, a standard four-digit code has been used by the U.S. government to identify the industries according to their products or services; this is the Standard Industrial Classification (SIC). These codes have become popular and have been adopted by many countries worldwide. For example:

- IBM is in the computer services industry, with a 7371 code.
- Starbucks is in the consumer services, restaurants, and bars industry, with a 2095 code.
- Boeing aircraft is in the aircraft manufacturing industry, with a 3721 code.

These codes are used to improve categorization and communication between various business and countries. It is now also obvious that each industry has its own distinct business characteristics and thus vastly different financial structures and measurements.

Key Point

The investor will learn soon that financial ratios by themselves are almost meaningless, unless a company's ratios are compared with others in the same industry.

I do not expect you to memorize any SIC codes. But I do wish to impress upon you that comparing companies among totally unrelated industries will not help you to evaluate the financial ratios of your chosen company and thus will be unhelpful for judging the desirability of its stock.

Returning to the debt ratio mentioned previously, it should now be crystal clear that comparing the debt-to-net-worth ratios of IBM and Starbucks will yield fairly inconclusive results. The same logic applies to all other financial indicators based on their financial statements.

As explained further in Chapter 4, financial indicators show the relationship of one figure of a company's financial statement to another figure, either from the same financial statement or from another statement. Thus if you intend to buy company *A* stock, you should be familiar with the respective industry norm, reflecting the average value for that type of business.

Furthermore, you may wish to reference its competition in the same industry so you can conclude that your Company *A* is indeed superior to its competitors and to the industry norm. For details on information sources, please see Chapter 4.

At this time, you may begin to realize how critical it is to know an industry well, prior to plunking down your hard-earned money to buy stock in any company in that industry.

To make money in a stock, you must be conversant with the industry and learn as much as you can about all aspects of the business—sales, production, financing, and management, among other things. In addition you should confirm your understanding through financial indicators analyses of respective financial statements over a reasonable period of time. See Chapter 4 for a detailed discussion of this.

D. Maxim No. 2: Profit from One Chosen Industry or a Selected Few Industries

1. Focus on the Industry

In a nutshell, I encourage you to pick one industry, or at most two industries, at any one time, depending on your available time. Then you develop expertise on the major companies within these industries. Learn their business models, the competition, the supply and demand on the customer bases, the relationship of sales with respect to the economy, and all the other conditions that make those companies either profitable, or not.

Key Point

Now if you add an industry using this methodology to your portfolio, one at a time, you are truly benefiting from investment diversification.

Once you understand enough about any industry, you will begin to be able to recognize "noise" from the media, newspapers, magazine, television, and other information sources.

2. Read "Tips," Not "Garbage"

How do you know that you have become an expert regarding an industry or an investment area? An acid test is that when you read or hear from anybody commenting on "nonsense investment tips" in your chosen industry, you recognize them immediately for what they are. You would sit back, smile, and say to yourself "How sweet it is that you do not fall for those bogus tips."

Key Point

Believe me that feeling is wonderful, as meanwhile you wonder how many more innocent people would get hurt.

Time and time again, when investors jump into a company not knowing the industry (e.g., product trends, supply and demand, product pricing), these investors are always at a disadvantage, as they never know when to get into a stock and when to get out. They are simply gambling with their hard-earned money.

Here is another example of a "good" stock to buy for folks "outside the industry." You may recall that a company not long ago claimed that it had invented a drug to detect the HIV virus. A person needed only to put this pill into a cup and spit into it to tell instantly whether he or she had the HIV virus simply by a color change in the pill. The potential was huge, thus the expected frenzy in buying into this stock. But a basic expert in this field would just smile at the world for being so naive and would move on without becoming a sucker.

Action Plan

1. Once you know a certain industry well and have a basic knowledge of it, track a handful of companies, say three, but preferably not more than five, depending on how much time you can afford for doing homework. If you try to follow too many companies, you probably would not have a sharp enough focus. Once you decide on the right prices to buy, you just wait for the right timing to get in, or simply stay out in cash. Often, not acting is the best action.
2. Study your focus industry for a period of time, say for one year depending on your personality and available time, but preferably not less than three months. You need time to dig into an industry, to study supply and demand, and to learn the terminology and basic industry structure.
3. This industry focus principle has been working for at least the 10 years during which I have been advising my friends. If this works for them, I am sure this will work for you as well.
4. Before taking any investment action, one should honestly ask oneself, "Am I really investing or am I really gambling? Is this excitement from investing merely a form of entertainment for me?" Based on years of observation, "investing as a game or entertainment" attitudes rarely produce profits consistently. I urge my readers to separate investment from entertainment totally.

Chapter 3

Wise Use of Information Resources

Should You Follow Hot Tips?

Try to distinguish between a stock commentary and true sound investment advice; take time to evaluate future long-term investment opportunities!

A. Listen to a Friend or Relative

Don't just listen to a stock name with a sensational story and invest right away. Do be critical, because the tips you receive may be good only very temporarily. Recall that in my story in Chapter 1, Joe was a "good friend," and I listened and responded to his hot tip. As a result, as a young man investing in the stock market for the first time, I lost 25% of my net worth in four weeks.

What we should be aware of is that when we trust a "good friend" or a relative as a person, that trust carries over to a "good stock." I was just following human nature, thinking

- I could be miserable if I did not buy the stock, as I might have missed a golden investment opportunity. I thought his information was valuable and adequate enough for me to make a decision.

- I felt obligated to my "friend" because I wanted to help his business (assuming this relative or friend is in the investment sales business).
- He might dislike me if I had not taken action because he was convinced of the reliability of his recommendation.

With any stock investment, it is almost like imagining yourself in a maze, with so many things to consider prior to a successful outcome. Therefore, I highly recommend that before any investments are made, you cool down to do some homework before you invest your hard-earned money. Do have entry and exit plans with any investments.

For example, what should your entry price be? What is your expected return? How long do you wish to hold? What is your target selling price? Or if the stock goes the other way, do you have a loss expectation price for you to exit at? In other words, you must have a plan for your investment, regardless of how approximate it may be.

With any investment, like everything else in life, you must expect the price to go up or down, probably reflecting certain economic cycles. No investment can go up forever without some adjustments or fluctuations, so have an exit plan at purchase time. You may modify it later, if necessary, as market conditions warrant.

As the nature of stock price fluctuations is industry-specific (see Chapter 2), each company's stock price volatility will generally follow certain characteristics of the industry. Thus, if you buy stock in a given industry, you need to place yourself in the appropriate "thinking mode."

For example, certain industries historically may display relatively narrow stock fluctuations (e.g., the utilities). Depending on your personal risk profile, for a medium-term exit plan you may wish to set a stop loss of, say 5% to 7%, either mentally or with a broker. However, because certain industries may historically register large price fluctuations (such as real estate and high technology), your medium-term exit plan may need to be set higher, say, 10% to 12%, depending again on your risk profile and investment horizon.

Moreover, because each investor's risk tolerance differs, acceptance of a certain degree of loss of principal would also be different. (Please see Chapter 4 on company analysis and Chapter 5 on portfolio management.)

It is perfectly natural to invest in stocks based on the comments of friends and relatives. This is totally understandable as the investor has already built up trust in his or her other areas of daily living with these same people. Therefore, the investor is already convinced that his or her friend or relative would not purposely recommend a "bad" stock. For stock value judgment, please see Chapter 4.

Key Point

Unless your friends or relatives truly have successful past investment records, you must separate relationship trust from investment return.

B. Listen to a Stock Guru

We have constantly been informed of possible good investments by stock gurus on TV and in magazines, newspapers, and other media. Often, we were excited by their recommendations. We rushed into taking their recommendations and invested. We were afraid to miss the opportunity to make quick money.

The truth is, time and time again, if any asset is a truly good investment, the trade-off of missing certain small price appreciation may be justified, as you need a little time to do some basic homework. It's better to be late and right, than to rush in and lose money.

The reality is that any media must continue to attract customers every day. Even though a certain stock or industry may be very good to customers, say on five contiguous days, media must change its "menu" daily so that information can be varied and new.

As discussed in Chapter 2, investors need to do homework and know their chosen industry well to make money. Most individual investors do not have the vast research resources of the big boys. Thus, individual investors must refrain from the temptation to be guided by the daily bombardment of "good stocks" announced by the media.

Key Point

With a truly good stock investment, one can still make good money over an extended period of time. In any case, it's better to take the time to be right than to rush in prematurely and lose your hard-earned money.

Examples include Johnson & Johnson, Apple, Google, Exxon, Caterpillar, McDonald's, Walmart, and other great companies. Historically, situations were never so rushed that if you missed a few days, you could never catch up. As you may realize, even with a strong and successful company, there will always be price fluctuations. Thus you would almost always have an opportunity to buy in your way at your price.

On the other hand, media stock stars, as good as they are, may not always be able to present you with the pertinent information you need to make a decision. They may recommend a stock without truly divulging details and critical information about the stock. Often, they should not be blamed for the quantity of information. Generally speaking, they have really limited time (or space) to explain all the details, due to the time (or space) limitations of a particular media program. You can imagine that these media stars may need to cover many stocks in a very limited time frame to appeal to many viewers.

For example, the media star may recommend an IT company with a newest product in computing technology. Although this star may have tons of technical information (and it all can be very truthful), they cannot be totally communicative due to time and space constraints. Furthermore, the stock price may not continue to do well inasmuch as numerous other factors can affect the resulting prices, such as strong forthcoming competition, government regulations, or the overall internal management of the company.

In all fairness, instead of criticizing the media stars, you should thank them. You may benefit by collecting their hot names and start doing your own homework to either concur with or dispute the stock recommendation before undertaking your proper purchase actions.

C. Listen to a Stock Analyst

Another pitfall is that we often rely on recommendations from stock analysts from large banks and brokerage houses. As we all know, these institutions must continue to recommend stocks from their research departments' analysts. Their survival depends on the relative success of their recommendations to the general public, among other factors.

Obviously, most of us do not have time to totally analyze a stock, due to work and/or family situations. We would rather take an easy way out than dig for information ourselves from many sources. It is tempting to just read one simple report from a famous institution. After all, these are highly paid investment professionals who are supposed to understand a company, an industry, or sectors.

Just as individual investors' personal situations are different, risk tolerance and investment time horizons are also different. A stock analyst probably could not recommend a stock based simply on so many personal investment profiles. By default, a stock analyst may only present to "all investors" a general recommendation. Thus, based on a very general "recommendation," an individual investor needs to adjust media information, such as buy–sell prices, stock holding period, and so forth. As you read these analyst reports, you should be asking:

- How many investors have already read the report?
- How many investors have already bought or sold the stock?
- By the time you read this report, have the company's conditions changed or has the industry trend changed?

In short, even if you get a quality report on a stock from the media, you still must follow my recommendation set down in Chapter 2: Invest in only one industry (or maybe a few, depending on how much time you can devote to homework). Only after you are quite familiar with the industry can you truly optimize the salient points from the analyst reports.

Analyst reports generally have numerous levels of recommendations. For discussion purposes, let us categorize using four levels.

1. Buy
2. Outperform the market
3. Hold
4. Sell

You may wish to gather statistics on these various recommendation categories. Analysts generally rate companies favorably, favoring "buy," "outperform the market," or "hold" and may be reluctant to rate "sell" unless the companies in question are truly experiencing material adverse changes.

Generally speaking, most analysts are capable and professional. Nevertheless, investors should account for human factors and judge accordingly. Again, their hard work to highlight certain stocks should be appreciated. At this point you might do additional homework on these stocks for your own benefit.

Key Point

My suggestion is that you should continue to read and benefit from these analyst reports. I am also reminding you that you must be aware of the roles they play and their own objectives.

D. Listen to an Investment Advisor

Investors may seek help from financial advisors (planners, consultants, etc.) to assist in choosing their investments.

Most of these advisors have solid education and superior training and are very professional. Their assistance should simplify the investment process and help you to achieve your investment targets easily.

Selecting an advisor involves numerous considerations, and these have been covered profusely in many articles and books and on websites; accordingly, I do not repeat them here. However, I would still wish to highlight the following criteria:

1. Actual track record

Even though most advisors have documented educational and license credentials, you should inquire about their investment track records. Without invading their privacy unnecessarily, you may ask them to quote examples of their wins. You should also ask them about their decision process—the basics of what, when, how, and why. Anyone can conjure up a winning story and a fantastic result, but if you listen carefully to the details and the respective logic, you can learn a lot.

2. **Risk quantification**

   During the boom times of any stock market, almost everyone can become a stock guru. It is during difficult times that how one manages downside risks can qualify one to be a guru.

   I have been in this investment business a long time and have come across many investment prophets. Though many of them were accurate some of the time, it is too much to expect a human being to be right all the time. Instead, you should ask the advisors how they quantify the downside risks of their proposals and how they deal with those risks in case they happen. You can learn a lot about their effectiveness by discussing probable adversities.

3. **Fee structure**

   Generally speaking, most advisors are smart, work very hard, and deserve their fees. I totally endorse a reasonable fee structure, because they are worth every dollar you spend. While this may be obvious to all, I just wish to caution you about:

   - Fee structure in relation to the scope of services to be provided (e.g., consultation time amount and frequency, access to their research capabilities regarding your investment areas, etc.)

- Fee variation, if any, for investment products designed by the advisor's company compared with other institutions, as the pricing of proprietary products may be influenced by internal policies
- Extraordinary high fees and structure in exchange for pie-in-the sky projected investment returns; evaluate any proposed merits based on fixed dollar vs. percentage fee structures?"

4. Compatibility

Get a gut feeling about the advisor after digesting related information and interviews. Deep down, you must have a feeling of trust as to whether or not you can depend on the advisor.

E. Listen to a Large Investor (Possible Shark)

Promotional tips for average investors could frankly come from anyone with deep pockets, so they can wind up with "deeper pockets." In other words, such tips could come from any large investor wishing to set up a money-making scheme.

I wish to quickly add that most large investors are good people and have good hearts. They wish to share their knowledge so small investors can benefit. Just beware of a certain minority of

Figure 3.1 How Sharks Work

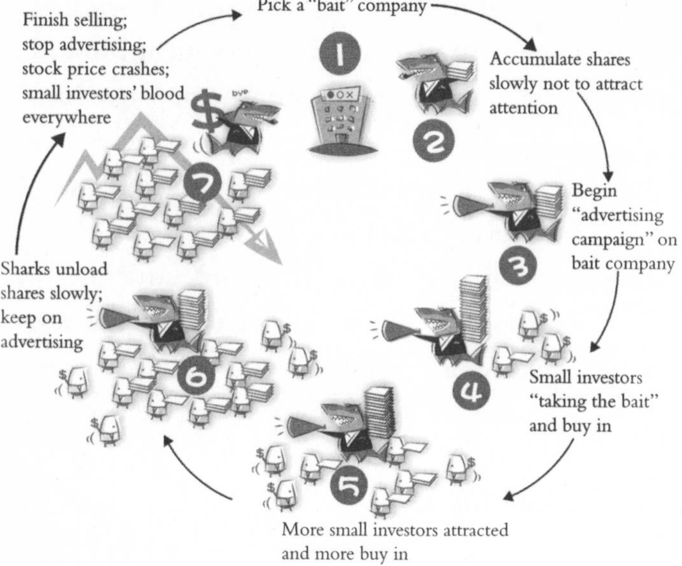

not-so-good ones. The scenario would go approximately like this (see Figure 3.1):

1. They pick a "bait" company.
2. They accumulate target shares slowly so as not to startle the market.
3. They begin a series of advertising campaigns, often using the traditional news mechanism in various media channels: newspapers, magazines, TV, and the Internet. The stock price would rise and small investors are sucked in.
4. The stock prices rises and small investors are sucked in.
5. As prices rise, more small investors are attracted.

6. They continue advertising until a "frenzy" price jump occurs, while beginning to sell their stakes slowly (to get the prices they want).
7. After all their shares are unloaded, price support advertising actions would cease.

Often, the upward momentum would continue for a while. Then it takes some industry or macroeconomic bad news to trigger a fall.

When that happens, this stock would crash, badly, because no buyers would come in, realizing then that the stock was way overbought. This plotline is similar to a fire in a building; everyone wants to get out at once. Then there is a lot of crying and yelling and panic everywhere, resulting in tragic outcomes for those trapped.

Now you may say, "this will not happen in my country." Think again. The possible truth is that these schemes could be carried out in many developed and emerging countries, with different "packaging" skills being applied.

I am amazed at how these "sharks" have gobbled up the money from small investors again and again. Blood and more blood is shed along with suffering and more suffering. This is happening even as I am writing this text.

Now you may ask, "What should I do, as a small fish?" The answer is, "Don't swim with the sharks in their own waters." The ocean is huge, so choose the water you know how to swim in. In other words,

choose the industry that you know well and in this way function to your best advantage.

You may wish to review Chapter 2 so you can tell when you come across a bogus "opportunity" for a certain industry. In Chapter 4, I discuss a simple framework for judging a company.

Several years ago, I was the chief investment officer (CIO) for a multi-asset diversified portfolio of approximately $2 billion. On an institutional portfolio basis, this size would not be classified as "large," but it's still sizeable compared with individual investors.

Many large portfolio managers do not proactively wish to affect an asset price. But since their transactions are usually larger than those of individual investors, their buy–sell orders would become noticed. Large portfolio managers often sense that small investors would follow them, wishing to tag on to their "trend" and profit on a short-term basis.

As institutions set a course of buying and selling, they often follow a set of portfolio objectives and execution criteria. They may also change course when macroeconomic or company conditions change. Thus, most institutions have sympathy for small investors, as they chase prices "in the dark." Meanwhile, institutions are proactively adjusting their investment plans and influencing the market prices, though not necessarily in a mischievous manner.

I can speak for my fellow CIOs by saying that most of us are executing our orders as normal activities. Yet asset prices do get affected simply due to our order size, dwarfing the traditional order size from individual investors.

Key Point

I repeat that an individual investor must study an industry well and do appropriate homework. One should select only a handful of stocks in that industry. Information from institutions or the marketplace should be used for reference only; alternatively, just laugh at it and move on. Preserve and protect your hard-earned money.

F. Maxim No. 3: Reference External Inputs but Stay Focused

Simple Profit Target Plan

As an example, many people feel a 7% to 10% return within a year is a good return. If this is your goal, then you should stick to your own plan. However, one may aim at an even higher return while accepting the risks associated with respective targets.

Obviously, price fluctuations may depend on numerous characteristics of a stock, such as the nature of the stock and the macroeconomic situation. At the same time, we recommend that you set a stop loss for any investment, depending on the type of that investment—for example, 5% depending on your risk appetite. In my years of making investments, I have seen many savings that were dissipated, resulting in broken families and personal fortunes lost, all due to unwillingness to admit a mistake. Even the best investment gurus make mistakes from time to time.

The important point is that they all recognized when the mistakes were made. They then devised action plans to get out with minimal loss. Professional investment managers make buy–sell decisions almost every day based on their preparation, research work, and judgment. One should think positively about mistakes, treating them as ways to pay tuition.

Key Point

Once having got out and learned the lesson, one should never look back and demoralize oneself. Always stay positive, always moving forward.

Do Simple Homework

I highly recommend that you do some basic homework on a company so that you know what you are investing in. After all, you are risking your hard-earned money.

Do look at the positive and negative sides of the company, even though it is presumably destined to be a successful company. Ask common sense questions such as What is the company's major competition? and Will a competitor be strong enough to affect the company's earnings materially?

A company may sound like a good investment target because it is in a promising industry, but it could get us into trouble if we do not learn the most basic marketing trends and financial numbers relating to that company.

For example, we may learn of a company with rich mineral resources in precious metals. Given the ongoing trends, gold, silver, and other precious metals are hot investing targets, especially when inflation is a threat. A mining company can become very profitable in riding this commodity trend.

However, one should try to learn some basic financials of a mining company. A company may have high-risk conditions; for example, it may borrow too much money to finance its mining equipment. Any unexpected future cash flow shortfall could expose the company to dangers of having insufficient funds to pay the interest on its bank loan, leading to possible serious financial distress. By way of example, due to the recent rampant printing of money by numerous central banks, precious metals (especially gold) investing has been very trendy.

Many ways are available to capture the expected higher gold prices; one of the popular ways is to invest in gold-mining companies. Even though we may be convinced that gold prices will increase, having the basic information about the gold-mining business would certainly help investors to choose the more promising companies.

Many factors could affect the success of a gold-mining company. For example, I cite the following three fundamental issues facing gold-mining companies for your reference.

1. Environmental issues

In the process of mining and refining gold, poisonous by-products may deliver serious consequences to the environment. Among numerous methods, cyanide heap leaching is one of the cheapest ways to extract gold. This process leaves behind toxic materials that contaminate the surrounding environment.

Cyanide is a deadly chemical, and major exposure of it to humans may cause damage to brain, heart, and other organs, leading to coma or even death.

Mercury is another chemical widely used in gold mining. Mercury vapor has been known to cause kidney and liver diseases in humans and animals. Even water contamination is a major gold mining issue. If polluted water enters into lakes and rivers, all living organisms can be affected.

If respective governments demand that the mining companies invest heavily to control or reduce these pollutants, the production costs would substantially increase, resulting in reduction of operating profits and eventually of stock prices.

2. **Miners' rights**

   Gold miners throughout the world are increasingly organizing to defend their rights regarding health and safety. For some larger gold mining countries, miners' health issues are the major reasons for strikes, which significantly affect the efficiency of gold production.

   As governments push for workers' rights, costs would escalate due to injury compensation, medical benefits, and associated safety practices.

3. **Financial structure**

   Given that a typical mining company needs a great deal of investment in land, plant, and heavy equipment, it is not unusual for it to float bonds or borrow heavily from banks.

For fast-growing mining companies, it is quite common that the liabilities increase faster than the return of cash flow. When expected cash inflow does not materialize, the highly leveraged company would face liquidity issues.

In a nutshell, I have just highlighted some pertinent operating issues faced by a gold-mining company. I would recommend that my readers learn the basic operating issues of any target company as common to the particular industry. For the mining industry, you may wish to look into country risks, such as the political environment, security/reliability of contracts, expropriation potential, and the likelihood of any corrupt practices, etc.—all of which may affect the stock prices of the companies. This way, when you invest your hard-earned money, you are well aware of the company's issues and associated opportunities.

We must discipline ourselves that we get to know the basics of a company and understand its business, as we explain further in Chapter 4.

Action Plan

1. Do not just simply listen to a "good" name with a sensational story and invest immediately because you feel that you might lose a great investment opportunity. Behind every message there may already be a position.
2. Do have a basic understanding of a stock, such as the company's basic competitive edge and most basic financial numbers.
3. Question whether such a company stock's desirability represents a fad or a truly new economic trend that you can benefit from for a long time.

Chapter 4

Decide on Company Values and Buy–Sell Prices

Should You Trust a Company with Your Money?

Learn the basic facts about a company's history. In other words, "trust but verify."

A. Relevant Company Historical Facts

Invest in proportion to how much you can trust a company with only minimal verification.

One of the key messages of this chapter is to avoid impulse investment. With your hard-earned money, it is crazy to just buy a stock and then hope and pray that the stock will make money for you. The often-practiced buy, hold, and pray (BHP) method, done without any homework, just does not work well, at least for most investment targets.

I am sure you have heard big win stories at dinners and cocktail parties. Your friends would boast of the huge profits they made in recent days (e.g., doubled their money in 10 days). However, I am sure you have not heard any of them letting you know about the huge losses they took using the BHP method without any verification.

1. Stock Prices versus Events

Following the logic of Chapter 2, after you have selected one industry and several stocks to track, go on to learn the history of these companies well, or as well as your time allows. This includes stock price changes for at least three years, with a recommended time frame of five years or more.

During that period of time, evaluate the stock price and respective trading volume changes with respect to the significant events in that period. You can get company information from many sources—prospectuses, annual reports, and numerous media sources. Let us start with general economic factors.

In the United States alone, reportedly there are a total of 80 macroeconomic indicators, the more popular ones being

- Consumer price index (CPI)
- Purchasing managers index (PMI)
- Gross domestic product (GDP)
- Payroll numbers
- Unemployment rates
- Housing starts
- Retail sales
- Consumption statistics

- Inventory levels
- Business confidence
- Consumer confidence

In any case, to understand your company, try to discover whether the company's stock prices were changed relative to certain economic indicators. Generally speaking, certain economic indicators may provide valuable clues to understand how other investors view the impact of these indicators on the company's financial health.

For example, if you are tracking a company that produces consumer products, the macro-indicators such as consumer confidence and retail sales figures may have certain effects on the company. But if you are tracking a heavy equipment manufacturer, then indicators connected to business confidence and inventory levels may be more closely related.

After focusing on the general indicators, study the indicators specific to your chosen industry. For example, if you are tracking an airline company, oil price fluctuations may affect its operating cost (or at least the perception of it) which then affect an investor's view of the airline's earnings and stock price.

The next tracking level to consider is changes specific to the company, such as announcement of

- Major management changes (to CEO, CFO, CMO, CIO, or other key management posts)
- Mergers or acquisitions of new businesses

- Major restructuring of the company's business products or services
- Staff reorganization (e.g., major additions or mass lay offs)
- Significant lawsuits that may affect the company's sales or profits
- Unexpected over performance or under-performance of expected earnings as estimated by financial analysts

To obtain information you need for simple homework, here is a list of sources for your reference.

1. Publications, some of which are tabulated here:
   a. Magazines
      - *The Economist*
      - *The Kiplinger Letter*

- *Bloomberg Businessweek*
- *SmartMoney* magazine

b. Newspapers

- *Wall Street Journal*
- *Financial Times*
- *Barron's*
- Local newspapers in major cities

c. Newsletters

- *Morningstar*
- *Value Line Investment Survey*
- *Standard & Poor's Stock Guide*
- *Hulbert Financial Digest*

2. Internet (some websites are listed here):

a. General or basic

- Yahoo! (www.yahoo.com/finance)
- Google (www.google.com/finance)
- Businessweek (www.businessweek.com)
- Bloomberg (www.bloomberg.com)

b. Information with informative stock charts:

- Big charts (www.bigcharts.com)
- Stock charts (www.stockcharts.com)
- Seeking Alpha (www.seekingalpha.com)

c. Brokerages and other financial institutions:

- Fidelity (www.fidelity.com)
- Schwab (www.schwab.com)
- E*trade (www.etrade.com)
- Market Watch (www.marketwatch.com)
- The Street (www.thestreet.com)

3. Company sources (some basic information is given here):

   a. Websites:

      Generally speaking, you may access the company's website by typing in its name or stock symbol, for example

      - www.exxon.com
      - www.caterpillar.com
      - www.ibm.com

      Click the tab for "Investor Relations" and then click information on financials or similar tabs.

   b. Annual reports:

      You may request these reports either through their websites or by phone, usually through their investor relations departments.

   c. SEC filings:

      You may access these detailed reports by going to company websites: Click "Investor Relations" and then "SEC Filings" for specific forms, such as 10K (annual reporting) or 10Q (quarterly reporting).

As a general note, as you plow through these various sources you may feel you have too much information instead of not enough. You will soon find that certain sources of information are more useful to you than others. In that case, you may choose to use these same sources repeatedly for various companies that you picked for homework.

Now you will begin to understand a company's stock price history and have learned how stock prices can be affected by numerous company events and economic conditions. You will try to make sense of the prices and respective trading volume and use that as a guide for buying in or selling out your positions.

Key Point

Remember, you can buy into the best stock in the world and still lose money if you do it at the wrong time.

---

2. Economic Events

I am reminded of Brian, a lawyer who believed that the fast food industry was a great industry and could not lose money. However, he bought the largest companies in this industry at a wrong time and still lost money in the short term. Why?

Since the October 1973 OPEC oil embargo and the ensuing oil shortage year of 1974, when gasoline prices hit the roof, many consumers chose not to go out and eat, because that required driving, among other factors. Most large companies in the fast food industry suffered sales declines as did their stock prices. For a long time even after 1975, these companies' stock prices did not recover materially.

However, at the writing of this chapter (mid-2012) the price of oil is around $85–100 per barrel. With the current economy finally adjusted to these "reasonable" oil prices, fast food companies are doing well again, and so are their stock prices.

The reason I mentioned Brian's story is that even with great companies in a growth industry, if they are not bought at the right time, one still could lose money over a short or medium time frame. Of course, if you hold a stock over a very long time, you probably would do well, assuming the company keeps up reasonable profitability and growth comparable with the overall industry. Depending on your investment time horizon, you may wish to hold a good stock for a long time despite temporary setbacks. (See Chapter 5 for a discussion of portfolio management.)

Key Point

You should select three companies within the chosen industry (maximum five), and track their stock prices as to how they varied as a result of major economic and company events. Record or memorize them. They will be useful reference points in determining your buy–sell prices.

---

3. Financial Events

Another example is the banking industry. We may recall the 2008 global financial crisis, which affected even the most influential banks in the world. Elton, a CEO of a real estate company, worshipped bank stocks. He invested heavily in them in 2007 and thought that these stocks would continue to appreciate significantly.

However, he did not take time to study the histories of banks as to how new financial changes might affect the banks' positions, such as the higher risk activities from their banking operations involving derivatives. At the writing of this chapter (mid-2012), most major banks' stock prices have not yet recovered from their levels in early 2007.

If Elton had done even minimal industry homework, he would easily have learned that banks are more vulnerable to global financial events, as they are relatively linked together through inter-bank mechanisms.

Beginning approximately in 2005, let us look at the major new revenue-producing areas of major banks. As derivative-based products yield relatively higher profit margins, numerous large global banks compete in devising and selling these new products to their clients.

As clients also competed for higher investment returns, they engaged more in derivative products such as structured notes, especially during the years 2005–2007. Then the 2008 global financial crisis hit, and both banks and clients suffered tremendously as some of those derivative risks exploded and devastated many balance sheets.

Let us cite another example of the interconnectedness of large global banks, the LIBOR fixing topic in 2012. LIBOR stands for London Interbank Offering Rate, a rate determined by major banks at 11 A.M. on banking days in London, the interest rate basis on which banks would lend funds to each other.

Thus, when the "fixing issues" were alleged by regulators, many large global banks were named as potential culprits. At the writing of this chapter (late 2012), these issues had still not been clarified or resolved.

In any case, Elton should have followed his chosen industry (banks) and done proper homework to understand the characteristic issues among major banks and would have been better prepared to avoid his losses accordingly.

In the following few sections I introduce certain key financial indicators, with the objective of assessing financial risks. Other pertinent characteristic features of a stock, such as dividend policy, will not be discussed here; such features border on investment styles, which vary with individuals.

For example, certain groups of investors prefer to profit from capital gains from stocks, whereas other groups prefer high dividends or dividend growth. Whether one style is better than the other depends on a number of factors, such as an investors' age and personality, the macroeconomic climate, and interest rate scenarios, among other things.

For example, for certain risk-averse investors, buying high dividend–paying stocks as a basic strategy certainly has been known through the years as a reliable methodology. I have recommended it highly to retired investors, for instance, and combining the maxims in this book, they have done very well, saving relatively the wear and tear of mental stress involved in dealing with the stock market.

I encourage these investors to familiarize themselves with this strategy by reading good books on it, as detailing the pros and cons here would be beyond the scope of this book. (You may reference Appendix D for an introduction to investing in high-dividend stocks.) For a discussion of portfolio risk management, please see Chapter 5.

B. Most Basic Financials

Be aware of a company's most basic financial information. Regardless of how little time you wish to spend in evaluating an investment, don't ignore simple financial figures and ratios and their implications.

In my management training program in New York, I was trained to run 36 ratios from the three typical financial statements (balance sheet, income statement, and cash flow statement). See Box 4.1 for a sample of these ratios.

Box 4.1: Sample List of Financial Ratios Useful in Understanding a Company

Most of you are not expected to spend time learning all these ratios; that's why you bought this book. However, if you want to drill down to the core structure of a company, this list is provided for your reference.

Group A: From Income Statement

1. Sales growth rate percentage
2. Gross profit margin percentage
3. Net income before tax divided by sales
4. Net income after tax divided by sales [NIAT/sales]
5. Interest expense divided by gross profit
6. Non cash expenses divided by gross profit

Group B: From Balance Sheet

1. Current ratio
2. Acid test ratio
3. Debt divided by total equity
4. Debt divided by total tangible net worth
5. Working capital (current assets minus current liabilities)
6. Current liabilities divided by total tangible net worth
7. Accounts receivable turnover (days)
8. Accounts payable turnover (days)
9. Inventory turnover (days)

Group C: From Cash Flow Statement

1. Net cash flow from core operations
2. Net cash flow from core operations divided by total net cash flow

(*continued*)

Group D: Cross-Statement Analysis

1. Return on assets (NIAT divided by total assets)
2. Return on capital (NIAT divided by tangible net worth)
3. Total sales divided by total assets
4. Gross profit divided by tangible net worth
5. Interest expenses divided by total debt
6. Net cash flow from core operations divided by sales
7. Net cash flow from core operations divided by total assets

Based on these ratios, among other inputs, we were asked to formulate our lending decision.

I do not expect you to learn and interpret all these; you are busy with many other more important activities in your life. However, I do recommend that you have a minimum understanding of a company's key ratios to the extent your time allows. Please note that this is the only place in this book I ask you to be familiar with some investment terminology.

C. Five Key Indicators

The five following indicators would be the minimum I would recommend you to understand, among certain others, depending on the industry. (Note: There are at least 68 major

industries/sectors. To discuss the particular financial behaviors of all of them would be beyond the scope of this book. Thus this recommendation primarily applies to our most common traditional companies.)

I wish to quickly note that anyone can easily pose another "five key indicators" that would be just as good if not better in assessing a company's

---

Key Point

These five financial indicators are my preferred choices for a high-level assessment of an organization's financial health. If you feel another five indicators are more helpful to you, that's fine too. Just ensure that your five indicators cover the essence of a company's financial health, at least for initial screening purposes.

My purpose here is to limit key ratios to a manageable number, as you may be short of time. Another concern is that I do not wish to drown you in a sea of figures that demand your patience and time. Obtain these figures for at least three years (the more the better to get a trend). Doing homework that covers five years is good, but probably there's no need to exceed seven, unless the company has volatile financial conditions.

---

health. Company analysis is often more an art than a science (see Box 4.1).

If your company is a non industrial company, you may wish to include three to five additional ratios to assist your assessment. However, I do caution you not to add too many indicators, because you may not reap the benefits of getting the "feel" of the pertinent messages that derive from the indicators.

For a simple illustration of financial ratios, I shall use a set of highly simplified financial statements of ABC Company (see Box 4.2).

Because readers may have various understandings of financial accounting terms, I shall briefly explain the terms in these statements (see Box 4.3). (More sophisticated readers might want to skip the following explanations.)

Box 4.2: Highly Simplified Financial Statements

(ABC Company 2013)

(Current Year for Illustration Only)

INCOME STATEMENT

Sales	$200M	
COS	$140M	COS = Cost of Sales
Gross Profit	$60M	
Expenses	$40M	
NIBT	$20M	NIBT = Net Profit before Tax
TAX	$5M	
NIAT	$15M	NIAT = Net Profit after Tax

BALANCE SHEET

Assets		**Liability + Net Worth**	
Current Assets	$60M	Current Liability	$30M
Non-current Assets	$40M	Non-current Liability	$40M
		Total Liability	$70M
		Net Worth	$30M
Total Assets	$100M	Total Liability + NW	$100M

CASH FLOW STATEMENT

Cash Inflow from Core Operations	$200M
Cash Outflow from Core Operations	$190M
Net Cash Flow from Core Operations	$10M
Cash Inflow (non core activities) [from sale of headquarters building]	$60M
Total Net Cash Inflow	$70M

Box 4.3: The Three Most Common Financial Statements

1. Income Statement

Also known as a "profit and loss" statement (or simply P/L statement), this statement captures the operating sales, costs, expenses, and profits at different levels for a certain accounting period, such as a month, a quarter, or a year.

I'll just highlight the key terms:

- Sales: From selling a company's goods or services
- Cost of sales (COS): total costs directly associated with those activities generating respective sales.
- Gross profit: sales less COS, a key measurement of the company's profitability before incurring other expenses.
- Expenses: after the gross profit level, numerous expenses must be incurred to support the operations, such as staff expenses, rental expenses, and other overhead expenses.
- NIBT (net income before tax).
- NIBT = gross profit less all other expenses.
- NIAT (net income after tax).
- NIAT = NIBT minus tax, also called "earnings" in the markets. When this NIAT figure is divided by number of shares outstanding, we have earnings per share (EPS), which is a popular indicator of a company's financial health.

2. Balance Sheet

This statement records the company's financial position at a point in time, such as end of month, quarter, or year.

- Current assets: assets generally deemed to be short term in nature, less than one year (e.g., cash, accounts receivable, inventory, etc.)
- Non current assets: assets generally deemed to be long term, more than one year (e.g., long-term investments, equipment, land, and buildings, etc.)
- Current liabilities: liabilities generally deemed to be short term, less than one year (e.g., accounts payable, short-term bank debts, etc.)
- Non current liabilities: liabilities generally deemed to be long term, more than one year (e.g., long-term bank borrowing long-term bonds, etc.)
- Net worth: difference between total assets and total liabilities, also known as stockholder's equity (e.g., original paid-in capital, retained earnings, etc.)

3. Cash Flow Statement

This statement captures cash flows of the operation for a certain accounting period such as a month, a quarter, or a year.

- Cash inflow and outflow from core operations, meaning cash flows from normal business activities of the company
- Cash flow (extraordinary), meaning cash flows from extraordinary or unusual events that are not part of the normal business, such as sale of a subsidiary company, or sale of real estate or buildings, and so forth

1. Derivation of the Five Key Financial Indicators

Sales Growth Percentage Try to determine whether the company's sales are increasing with respect to the industry and the economy. Obviously, the higher the better, in most cases.

To make this calculation, simply divide this year's sales by last year's sales. For example, if this year's sales amount to $200M and last year's sales amounted to $170M, growth would be 17.6% ($200M/$170M = 1.176).

Gross Margin Percentage Make sure that the gross margin percentage is at least the same for the current year if not increasing. I emphasis gross margin instead of net profit, as net profit can be relatively easier to be manipulated (e.g., by drastic reduction of staff, research, or advertising expenses for a short-term show of net profits).

Make this calculation by taking gross profit divided by sales (the higher the better). For example, if sales amount to $200M and gross profit is $60M, gross margin would be 30% ($60M/$200M = 0.30).

Debt-to-Net-Worth Ratio (D/E Ratio) You should also be aware when the company continues to borrow heavily with respect to its own industry.

Any sudden change in cash flows could jeopardize the company's stability by incurring disproportionate interest expenses.

Make this calculation by taking total debt divided by net worth (the lower the better). For example, if total debt is $70M and net worth is $30M, the D/E ratio = 2.33.

Net Cash Flow from Core Operations Try to learn how the company generates positive cash flow from core operations. Is the cash flow growing in line with the industry? Be sure to eliminate any one-time gains or losses from non core activities.

Make this calculation by netting out any one-time events (e.g., netting out cash from sale of building thus resulting in $10M in our example); generally, the higher the better.

Net Cash Flow from Core Operations Divided by Total Assets (NCFCO/TA) This is a good measure of the company's ability to generate net cash flow from its operations with its total assets. It provides a quick measure of the company's efficiency.

Make this calculation by dividing net cash flow from core operations by total assets. For example, $10M/$100M = 10% (the higher the better).

2. Initial Interpretation from Five Financial Indicators

Using the formula as stated previously, one can easily calculate the five key indicators.

Using some hypothetical figures from the previous two years (20×0, 20×1) and the figures just explained from 20×2, we may arrange them as shown here:

		20×0	20×1	20×2
1.	Sales Growth (%)	13.0	15.0	17.6
2.	Gross Margin (%)	25.0	28.0	30.0
3.	Debt/Net Worth (times)	1.50	2.00	2.33
4.	Net Cash Flow: Core Operations ($Mil.)	30	20	10
5.	Net Cash Flow: Core Operations/Total Assets (%)	20	15	10

Even though the figures are quite simple and hypothetical, they are useful for illustrating the most basic financial changes of ABC Company. We may deduce the following financial messages from this simple tabulation:

1. Sales growth has been healthy, with a positive increase every year from 13% to 15%, then to 17.6%. Though this indication is positive, one may inquire whether this is in line with competitors in the same industry.

2. Gross profit margin also looks healthy, increasing from 25% to 28%, then to 30%.

   This situation is also positive. But one should dig deeper into the major products of ABC if certain products command disproportionate higher gross profit margins. Can ABC continue this trend given its resources? Will market growth trend support these higher-margin products?
3. The D/E ratio has increased from 1.5 to 2.0, then to 2.33.

   Such debt leverage should raise some questions. If debt increase (versus retained earnings) is needed to finance growth, is it a weakness to be noted? Do other competitors also need to raise debt to finance growth?
4. Net cash flow from core operations decreased from $30M to $20M, then to $10M. Is this another weakness to check? One needs to dig deeper into ABC's cash flow statements. Remember that numerous accounting games can be played (and displayed) with financial statements.

   Before making any investment, one must identify the company's strengths and weaknesses. Among other figures, net cash flow from core operations is probably the least prone to the kind of "accounting packaging" that has been highlighted in this chapter.

5. NCFCO divided by total assets dropped from 20% to 15%, then to 10%. It appears that ABC is less efficient in generating cash from its assets. Again, more digging is called for. Try to analyze previous years; does this indicate a trend or is it merely a temporary occurrence?

We have just illustrated how these five key indicators can help to determine the relative financial strength of ABC Company, using highly simplified figures. As indicated previously, if necessary you can analyze further by using other ratios, such as the samples shown in Box 4.1.

Key Point

It is meaningful to compare your chosen company's financial ratios only with companies in the same industry. It is often useful to set up a table listing the same key financial ratios for competitors in the same industry.

Numerous financial websites offer a preset financial format. Certain websites may even provide competition companies (e.g., www.yahoo.com/finance). As of 2012, for example, to compare the major pharmaceutical companies, start with Merck, by entering MRK at "Get Quotes," and then click on "Competitors" under "COMPANY."

A preset financial format would emerge with Merck's key competitors as shown here:

GSK	GlaxoSmithKline plc
NVS	Novartis AG
PFE	Pfizer, Inc.
Industry Average	(major drug manufacturers)

For a chosen company, certain websites allow you to pick the competitor that you wish to compare on stock information (e.g., www.fidelity.com). As of 2012, after clicking the "Research" tab, click "Stocks," type "MRK" for Merck at "Enter Company or Symbol," and then click "COMPARE." Merck's key stock investment information will then appear. At the same time, four blank spaces would appear next to "MRK" (your company) and prompt you to enter the competitors that you want to compare. Then you may type in GSK, NVS, PFE, and so forth, after which corresponding stock information will appear.

You could try out various websites that were covered previously in this chapter to familiarize yourself with respective preset formats. If those websites do not show your favorite financial figures or ratios, you can easily set up a simple chart to track these figures using your favorite information sources.

If anything in this discussion does not make sense to you, you should reconsider your investments. At least, don't go crazy with your hard-earned money.

In the long run, cash flows and earnings determine market prices. However, investor sentiments often determine market prices in the short term. What we should focus on are true intrinsic values for longer-term horizons.

D. Don't Be Blind to a Company's Personality

Try to invest employing your own strategies. Most readers are familiar with evaluations of companies based on financial information. However, the nonfinancial information can be just as important in evaluating the company for your investment. In other words, knowing the company's culture should also be helpful in your evaluation.

As you might suppose, there are probably 101 ways to study the company's culture. One of the easiest ways to start is by observing the CEO's personality. In addition, observe changes of CEO within a company; CEOs come and go. During these changes, company cultures may or may not change. This may also be influenced by the company's board of directors, key executives, or other cultural factors engrained in the company.

When reading financial reports, let me remind you to learn to decipher the "soft speak" in any sentences in financial reports. Let us take a glove manufacturing company to make a point. To highly simplify the products, let us say that the company makes only two types of gloves—cloth and leather.

In a shareholder report, the CEO announces that the company will change to a "superior product strategy" (concentration on cloth glove production only). The decision was based on the much larger market for cloth gloves; thus sales are expected to increase. In addition, production worker resources and inventory management can now be significantly simplified, thus increasing overall efficiency.

On the surface, this is a positive announcement. However, the CEO did not volunteer other facts: the company was experiencing difficulty in selling leather gloves, and thus there was no point in continuing to manufacture them.

From a financial standpoint, the CEO also failed to mention that the gross profit margin of cloth gloves was only 10%, compared with 40% for leather gloves. Unless the future cloth glove sales can increase dramatically, the total gross profit will suffer, directly affecting net profit and stock prices.

Once you have identified any "soft-speak" language or oversimplified statements, it may be a signal for you to go slow and make your judgment accordingly.

E. Deciding on Buy–Sell Prices

To systematically determine your buy–sell prices, I would recommend that you follow the flowchart shown here (see Figure 4.1). The respective chapters are noted in each step to facilitate your review.

Notes on the Flowchart

1. In doing your homework, after reading Chapter 2 you will have finally chosen a target industry. Given the basic operating components or the

Figure 4.1 Flowchart to Determine Buy–Sell Prices

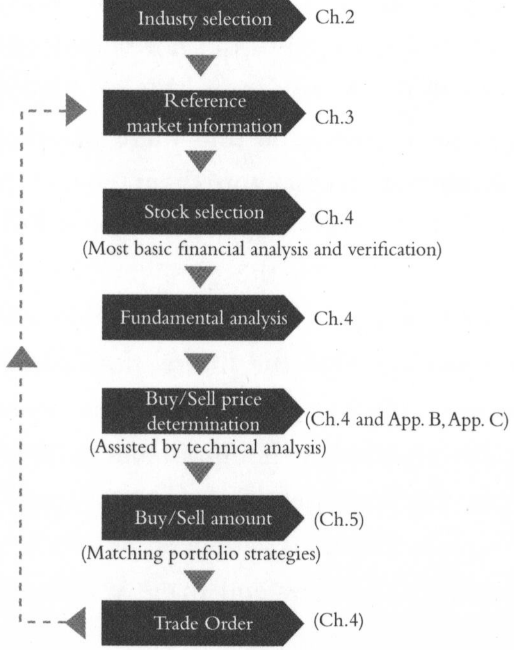

business models in the industry, you will begin to have good criteria for picking the better companies.

You will also note the major trends and risks that prevail in the industry. You may pick three companies as your investment targets on a relative basis—that is, which companies have better intrinsic values over their current stock prices.

2. After reviewing Chapter 3, you will begin to use certain media information for reference. You should now be able to distinguish "noise" from helpful insights.

   You will learn to filter media information and distill useful nuggets of information to initially set your future buy–sell prices.

3. As introduced in Chapter 4, you will confirm your sense of company financial conditions using super simple financial analysis via the five key ratios and figures. You can now rethink your initial opinion of the company and may further adjust the buy–sell prices (see Box 4.4).
4. After fundamental analysis, as discussed in Chapters 2, 3, and 4, you will also apply technical analysis to reconfirm your buy–sell pries within certain time frames (see Appendix A, Appendix B, and Appendix C).

There must be at least 100 books on technical analysis in the marketplace, so I won't go into

Box 4.4: Buy–Sell Tips

Among numerous creative types of orders, I highly recommend that you become familiar with good-till-cancel (GTC) orders to help you in managing your buying and selling prices. GTCs are available from many brokerage houses.

After doing your homework, you may wish to consider your selected entry price and enter a GTC buy order. This is especially helpful when the stock is too hot. You may wish to enter an appropriate price to fit your own profit projection.

When you decide to sell your stock, you may then enter another GTC sell order to exit your investment with your intended profit.

Obviously, no one type of trade order is perfect for all situations. For example, a traditional disadvantage of a GTC sell order is that if you set the respective sell price too close to a market price, a "professional trader" may engineer a buy order just to consummate your order, fairly or unfairly.

One must do appropriate homework on the nature of a stock (e.g., its historic price volatility) to set optimum buy–sell limits.

it here. However, after 40 years in the market, I would recommend using both fundamental and technical analyses to be successful. One should not rely on purely technical analysis and expect to make money consistently over the long term (see Appendix A).

F. Maxim No. 4: Trust but Verify

1. Most Basic Skills

Do develop basic skills if you can on financial statements, to the extent your time allows. However, given the limited time that you have, I would not expect you to be an expert on numerous financial indicators. What I am trying to do is to highlight these five financial indicators so you can consistently use them to screen out weaker targets and compare one company with another.

This process is not difficult. For example, Julia was a sales director of a clothing company. Although Julia was not financially trained, by making some minor efforts in her spare time she began to grasp the essence of these five key financial numbers easily.

After you have chosen a company, you should track the historical prices and volumes, noting how and how many major events affected them. These events might be external (e.g., global political events, macroeconomic changes, industry innovations, etc.). Internal company events might include announcements of major investments, new products, new mergers of partners, and so forth.

Depending on individual styles, you may simply note them on your own log book. Some may wish to put these statistics on the computer, using Word or Excel. The methodology is not important.

The key is to research them and record them, so they are available for future reference in deciding on buy–sell prices in the future.

I wish to emphasize that most individual investors are obsessed with stock prices, weekly, daily, or even hourly. Note that a stock price is simply a result of people auctioning in the stock market. Their emotions do play a major role in determining the price at any given time, rightly or wrongly.

I rather encourage you to pay more attention in developing your understanding of the fundamentals of your chosen company, with respect to its industry/sector. Prices are for reference only as to how your chosen stock is perceived by the masses. You should continue to develop your own feel and judgment of the intrinsic value of the company.

Prices will continue to be indicators of this ongoing auctioning process. As emphasized in this chapter in numerous places, the reliable value of a company is ultimately based on its ability to generate consistent cash flows from its core operations!

Obviously, past events do not guarantee the reoccurrence of changes of the same magnitude in the future. However, these exercises have repeatedly helped stock owners to buy to profit while others are sitting on the sidelines, and to sell to avoid major losses when others are still intoxicated by inflated prices.

After you have done your homework for a sustained period, you can feel sure that your judgments of price and volume data are in sync with actual market movements. Then you are ready to act in real time. If you still are not sure, do some paper trading for a short time (say four to six weeks) and check your degree of understanding of the company.

Key Point

Believe me, when you are ready, you will feel a surge of confidence while ignoring all the noise going around in the markets. Reaching that level will certainly bring you a sense of sweet victory and internal bliss.

---

2. Self-Interest

Whenever you read any financial articles, always question the authors' motivation. Why would the authors say what they say? Is there any self-interest involved? For example, why would an oil analyst suggest that oil prices might be going to $300 per barrel within two years? Why would a mining analyst forecast that gold would be $5,000 per ounce within three years? Of course, anything is possible in the future. Just bear in mind the author's possible self-interest. For example, if the author or spokesperson is a gold expert, you should listen carefully, given the expert's professional training and experience.

Learn to decipher the experts' ways of predicting future gold prices, especially when the prognostics are poor. It is never too late to learn how many ways experts can divulge "unpleasant" signals.

This prognostication is more an art than a science. Once you make this skill a habit, you'll never forget it. On the other hand, also learn how experts promote good news, especially given that gold prices were already at the $1,850 per ounce level in the third quarter of 2011.

I must be fair and state that most experts are professionals, and they genuinely wish to assist the public in making good investments. Still, buyers should beware.

Depending on the country, some governments are increasingly imposing disclosure laws and security practices on public communication. As a benefactor of these experts, you should be fully aware of the requirements of various security-related professionals, such as analysts, financial advisors, newspaper columnists, and part-time magazine article writers, among others.

Key Point

Remember: Behind every message, there may be a position.

---

3. View a Company as a Person

I highly recommend that you follow a company and attempt to view it as a person. Like a human being, each company has its own culture and its own business philosophy. When I was in corporate lending, I was fortunate to have my boss train me to judge a company both by its financial numbers and by its nonfinancial attributes such as personality.

I am sure that consciously or unconsciously you evaluate your own friends in a similar way. Based on these kinds of judgment, ensure that your investment strategy coincides with your perception of personality. This judgment could be helpful to you in determining your amount of investment on a relative risk basis.

Action Plan

1. Although you have limited time, I encourage you not to ignore the most basic financial figures of a company. I propose that you become familiar with a few basic financial indicators. A good start would be to use the five financial figures suggested previously. If you wish to add other meaningful indicators, please go ahead as long as you can focus on the key indicators of financial health.
2. Focus on the company's history and understand how its stock prices and respective trading volume have varied over time. This will give you an advantage in determining which price to use to get in and which to use to get out.
3. Make your own judgment of the personality of the company as you would with a person.
4. Behind every message, there may be a position.
5. Trust but verify.

Chapter 5

Simple and Effective Portfolio Strategies

Do You Want a Windfall Profit or a Systematic Win?

Do not disproportionally invest in any one stock or asset in one lump sum.

A. Portfolio Planning Guidelines

We all want to make a killing once and for all and then retire. However, this is a dangerous game. Once you concentrate your financial resources toward one single target, the risk of ruining your financial health can be very real indeed.

Temper Your Windfall Profit Desire with Systematic Wins

Throughout my investment years, I have observed all types of investors, from the smallest individual investor to CEOs of large global multinational companies. Whoever can make money consistently would follow a systematic process, some crude and some sophisticated.

Regardless of their methodologies, every year these investors would reliably make money, depending obviously on overall global conditions. Even with a consistent profit of 10–25% per transaction, they would achieve handsome profits by accumulating their "small" wins.

On the other hand, I also have known many bold investors who were always looking for that one-time big win. Obviously, we have all heard those anecdotes about "investment heroes" and "sensational stock gurus" and how they flipped a 100% to a 500% gain in just one deal. Average investors often worship them, dreaming that they will be the next and will earn a fame that could last for another 100 years.

But if you research these "heroes" and the conditions necessary to make the big win happen, you would conclude that the chance of success may resemble that of winning a national lottery.

Key Point

Build your own simple yet systematic methodology to make money consistently.

If you target smaller wins and achieve these repeatable wins year after year, is that so bad?

Before we discuss the proper structure of your portfolio, let us reiterate that you must decide based on your own family needs and personal style.

1. **Family needs**

   Let us cite two extremes:

   a. In the first extreme, you may be young and single and do not have any family members to support. If you lose your capital, you can still survive with your current income from your job.
   b. In the other extreme, you may be older and have numerous family members to support. If you lose your capital, it would create a hardship for now and also for future retirement. Besides, you might not know how long you could work because of instability of your position at your company or impending poor health.

   Obviously, there may be many individuals who fit between these two extremes. Thus, you need to assess your own family needs realistically.

2. **Personal investment style**

   Notwithstanding the foregoing examples, personal style also dictates our portfolio construction. Let us cite two most common types, which have many variations, assuming that both expect long-term gains in the stock market.

   a. The aggressive type expects to capture most (if not all) of the opportunities in the market. This style tends to experience more risk and more volatility.

b. The conservative type expects *not* to capture all opportunities in the market. Capital preservation is a paramount objective. Foreseeing any possible dangers, this type will not go ahead. Some positive gains will be missed, but the reality will be readily accepted.

Regardless of family situations and personal styles, we find these portfolio construction strategies beneficial, as discussed in the following section.

After spending 40 years in investing, one thing I did learn well is that there is no such thing as zero risk. Even the simple objective of preserving your capital in cash carries a risk, as inflation can easily impact the purchasing power of your portfolio.

B. Core versus Satellite Portfolio

Preservation of your fighting power is your key to long-term success.

The Need for Two Types of Portfolio

To separate your portfolio into two types of investment has been helpful: core portfolio and satellite portfolio. In a core portfolio, these are the safe, tried and confirmed dependable investments. These should make up the greatest percentage of your investments.

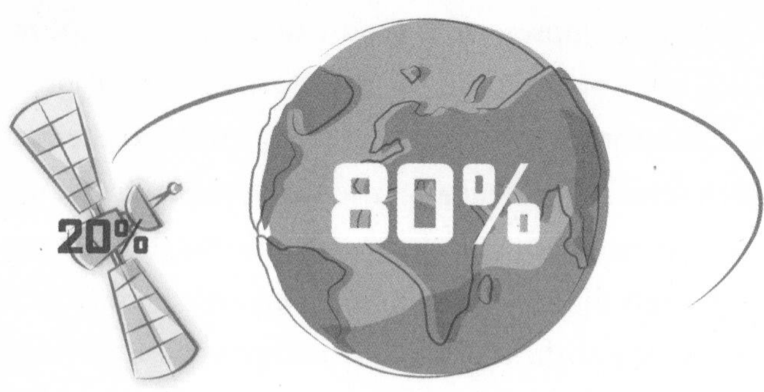

Given that investors have different risk profiles, it would be difficult to specify which assets or stocks to put in the core portfolios rather than the satellite portfolios. But the logic would be crystal clear for allocating a majority percentage of assets to your safer portfolio, say, 80%. As time and global conditions vary, obviously you can reset this percentage.

If you start out in cash, you might put aside 80% of the total amount in a safe place (e.g., an insured deposit account with a bank or in money market–type funds with a safe institution).

After performing due diligence, you would accumulate your positions in low-risk assets with this 80% cash. Depending on global conditions and your investment environment, you might decide on certain strong and stable stocks of blue-chip multinationals, bearing in mind what was said in Chapters 2, 3, and 4.

In a satellite portfolio, you should try out promising new investments. This is your laboratory or test-tube stage of investing. If they prove successful, these investments may be moved to your core portfolio to generate systematic wins. According to this logic, you might start with 20% to 30% of your total portfolio, depending on your risk acceptance levels.

Once you put assets into this satellite portfolio, you need to recognize the risks and track their performance closely. Just in case you feel risks are greater than you can accept, you need to get out, even at a loss, to stop the bleeding. After an appropriate observation period, you should rate your new assets regularly in your satellite portfolio as to whether they are dependable. If so, you may wish to move them to your core portfolio.

As to how often you set their probation periods, it depends on the asset type and industry along with numerous macroeconomic factors. As a guideline, you should review these investments on a monthly basis for the short term, setting a probation period of six months or one year. How you set these time periods is not critical; the important point is that review must be done regularly.

You may also wish to rebalance your assets regularly, based on, say, a 80/20 split on core-to-satellite percentage. For a simple example of rebalancing, Figures 5.1 and 5.2 are designed to illustrate this point.

Figure 5.1 Beginning Portfolio Combination

Core Portfolio (70%)

Blue Chip Stock A	5%[a]
Blue Chip Stock B	5%[a]
Blue Chip Stock C	5%[a]
Blue Chip Stock D	5%[a]
Blue Chip Stock E	5%
Blue Chip Stock F	5%
Blue Chip Stock G	5%
Blue Chip Stock H	5%
Other safe assets (E.g. low risk bonds)	25%
Cash	5%
Total	70%

Satellite Portfolio (30%)

Promising Stock M	5%[b]
Promising Stock N	5%[b]
Promising Stock P	5%[b]
Promising Stock Q	5%[b]
Promising Stock R	5%
Cash	5%
Total	30%

Note a: If you confirm that Blue Chip Stocks A, B, C, and D have shown deterioration due to poor growth prospects or worsening financial conditions, you would sell them and put the cash proceeds (equivalent to 20% of portfolio) in the satellite portfolio.

Note b: If you confirm that Promising Stocks M, N, P, and Q are indeed low risk, you should move them (equivalent to 20% of portfolio) into the core portfolio.

Note c: With this rebalancing, you now have 25% in cash in your satellite portfolio to buy new assets.

Figure 5.2 Portfolio after Rebalance

Core Portfolio (70%)

Blue Chip Stock E	5%
Blue Chip Stock F	5%
Blue Chip Stock G	5%
Blue Chip Stock H	5%
Promising Stock M	5%[b]
Promising Stock N	5%[b]
Promising Stock P	5%[b]
Promising Stock Q	5%[b]
Other safe assets	25%
Cash	5%
Total	70%

Satellite Portfolio (30%)

Promising Stock R	5%
Original Cash	5%
New Cash	20%[a, c]
Total	30%

Proper Percentage Guidelines

In most cases, I recommend placing 80% of your resources in a core portfolio and 20% in a satellite portfolio. Obviously, each investor has his or her own risk appetite. Some of you may opt for 70/30, some may even opt for 60/40. I would not recommend anything lower than 60/40, unless you have strong reasons to justify another arrangement

As you select the assets to put into the core or the satellite portfolio buckets, your target is to grow your money on a consistent basis.

Key Point

I wish to reiterate that your primary objective is to preserve your capital—that is, do not lose money or at least be ready to stop your losses if you happen to make some mistakes.

Therefore, you should build a portfolio model just for you. As you become reasonably competent in a certain industry and buy certain companies, you may then begin to diversify to another industry, always building your overall portfolio from strength to strength.

Now you are finally reaping the rewards of methodical diversification, unlike most smaller investors, who diversify from one type of sandcastle to another. Thus, they are diversifying blindly. You may argue that they derive some benefit from buying stocks from various industries. But look further beneath the façade; these investors did not really buy the best companies within the industries they chose, because they generally did not do the necessary homework. So when economic down cycles come, these "floods" will cause substantial damage to their diversified "sandcastles."

It should now be clear how to group your stocks or assets properly into two different buckets—core and satellite portfolios. But from time to time there may be personal favoritism in the way you view different stocks.

For example, you may find certain companies with high growth and probably both higher risk and higher reward. Their stocks should go into the satellite portfolio until they are "seasoned" or until you are sure that these companies warrant your placing them in your core portfolio.

On the other hand, there may be superior growth companies with proven markets and financial strength; you may wish to put them in your core portfolio. As you become more experienced, you may use your own personal criteria to select these companies.

For example, you may be the type of investor who favors stocks that provide reliable income, because of your age, family situation, or investment style. In this case, you may wish to add stocks with a long history of uninterrupted dividends, or better yet, uninterrupted increase in dividend rates (see Appendix D).

As a general rule, I recommend the following guidelines to deal with concentration risks for the number of stocks and industries in a portfolio. As a percentage of total portfolio, use the following:

1. For each stock, 1–2% in the initial phase, building up to 5% as a maximum target.
2. For each industry, 10% in the initial phase, building up to 20% as a maximum target. Please start with one chosen industry, then add another industry when you feel you have already mastered the first one. Then add one at a time, reaching a maximum of four to five industries over a long period of time. Total elapsed time will obviously depend on your time availability.

   Depending on your personal attributes, six months (full-time devotion) to two years (part-time) may be reasonable. (*Note*: Before you buy stocks in a particular industry, you should allocate your cash to safe investments (such as time deposits or other safe assets.) Over a period of time, you may build up your stock portfolio wisely.

C. Portfolio Risk Management

As the future cannot be predicted, the best we can do is to manage the risks that come with future uncertainty.

As much as possible, you should strive to learn the basics and acquire the ability to identify risk and possibly to measure it. Then you need to follow up with action plans to mitigate the risk, based on your knowledge of the consequences.

Numerous books have been written on risk management, and I encourage you to pick one and learn as much as your time allows. However, I would like to highlight some basic concepts critical to portfolio management just as a start, as detailed risk discussions are beyond the scope of this book.

Unfortunately, risk and reward go together. It is much easier to aim for high reward (return on investment) than to assess the associated high risks. But we must start some place.

Although overlapping risk factors do occur from time to time, let us address each major category separately. At least the next time you buy a stock (or any asset), you will be somewhat clearer in your own mind about the degree of risk you could be dealing with.

Now we pose a somewhat rhetorical question. Why do investors need to manage basic risks?

Key Point

Given the increasingly globalized factors affecting stock markets, interest rates, foreign exchange rates, and so forth, one cannot consistently predict future trends. Thus, through deliberate identification of risks and assessment of their respective magnitudes, one can proactively either avoid, transfer, reduce, or even accept such risks.

I have many friends who enjoy talking only about the profits of money-making grand schemes. They consider risk discussions as cowardly. Furthermore, they would belittle such discussions as a sign of a weakling mentality. However, most of my CIO friends believe that risk discipline should be an investment habit. If one happens to disagree, I would say "hats off" to these super-humans.

For each investment, I suggest that an investor should quantify the return and risks by asking the three most basic questions:

1. What is the return on investment (ROI)?
2. What is the exit time (days, weeks, months)?
3. What is the maximum loss contemplated?

Although a risk guru can highlight 16 or more different risks, I intend to concentrate on four major categories, which are further explained in the next few sections.

1. **Market risks:**
    a. Interest rate risk
    b. Foreign exchange risk
    c. Inflation risk
2. **Credit risks:**
    a. Liquidity risk
    b. Bankruptcy risk
3. **Operational risks:**
    a. People or employee risk
    b. Technological risk
    c. Settlement or delivery risk

4. **Legal and political risks:**
   a. Country legal system risk
   b. Political policies risk

As is often the case in the investment world, risks often occur in tandem. However, for the sake of clarity, we need to focus on them individually. This should remind you to examine these risk categories the next time you invest in a stock or any asset.

1. Market Risks

These are risks of loss resulting from changes in market conditions, such as interest rates, foreign exchange rates, inflation rates, and the like.

a. Interest Rate Risk Although this risk historically affects fixed-income securities more, stock prices often are correlated with interest rate changes in many countries. Generally speaking, as interest rates increase, investors move their money into fixed-income securities and other related areas to lock in interest income.

Obviously, for existing fixed-income instruments, if interest rates become higher, such prices would move in opposite directions.

b. Foreign Exchange (FX) Risk Remember that your stock currency should ideally be denominated in the same currency as your future cash outflow plans, otherwise adverse FX changes would materially affect your return on investment. Obviously, with strong cross-rate currencies against your home currency, you may gain on perceived appreciation potential, such as with the Chinese RMB or the Norwegian Kroner as of 2011.

c. Inflation Risk Because inflation would basically reduce your future purchasing power, it would be wise to account for this in your diversification of countries and areas so as to maintain your target returns on investment.

2. Credit Risks

These are risks of loss resulting from a change in credit quality of an asset, or a company's worsening credit position, leading to defaults or bankruptcy.

a. Liquidity Risk A company can be profitable, but still may incur liquidity risk. This is entirely possible when its cash inflow timing cannot match the required cash outflow. This often happens to a company with profitable operations based on accounting conventions, yet such companies might become cash-strapped, which could trigger a financial difficulty. Due diligence checking on balance sheet and cash flow ratios would be helpful.

b. Solvency or Bankruptcy Risk By means of simple financial analysis, one can obtain a reasonable feel for the financial health of a company (see Chapter 4). A credit rating from the credit agencies should provide a reasonable assessment. However, I would caution you *not* to rely solely on ratings. For example, before our most recent financial tsunami, Lehman Brothers had been rated AA. Now you could appreciate the fact that credit ratings can change really quickly.

As much as your time allows, do your own independent tracking, as you would have more time to exit a position prior to rating downgrades.

At my last CIO position, I had to monitor the credit ratings of many companies and act before actual changes occurred. For example, I had many world-class multinational bonds in my portfolio, with sales ranking within the top 5% in the world. These bonds have been known throughout the world as stable investments, appropriate for very conservative investors, due to their long histories.

For many years, these companies enjoyed a high credit rating, even as late as 2000, with A ratings or above. However, because of the deteriorating financial conditions of some companies, they were downgraded to B ratings (a non investment grade category) toward the end of 2005.

I still recall that numerous CIO friends had been systematically tracking these companies. They sold out their positions long before the actual downgrades occurred. At the time of the downgrade announcements, the market was stunned at the volatility prevalent in the investment world; even the bluest of the blue chips could be subject to a downfall.

3. Operational Risks

These are risks that occur due to operational breakdown due to people, process, computer, and technical factors.

a. People and Employee Risk Although it may be difficult as an outsider to track company employees, you should be aware of a company's relative reputation in matters of internal control. Stock prices generally suffer (at least temporarily) when employee risk incidents occur.

For example, you may recall the employee risk incidents in the recent past, from the Nick Leeson case at Barings Bank in 1995, the Jerome Kerviel case at Sociéte General Bank in 2008, and the Kweku Adoboli case at UBS in 2011. They are similar in that these traders exceeded their trading limits and incurred losses, creating either financial hardship or poor reputation for their companies. Stock prices obviously suffered as a result. Other employee risks may be to key employees' health or continuation of their employment."

b. Technological Risk Some companies rely on certain technologies to excel or to dominate their competition in their industries. If one of their competitors develops a more advanced technology, then others will suffer or be eliminated; thus, the technological risk.

For example, in the high-tech business, when Apple Computer Co. developed the touch screen and other previously unthinkable applications with its iPhone, other mobile phone manufacturers were greatly affected, as reflected quickly in their stock prices. Of course, technological innovations come swiftly, and companies need to continue to excel; otherwise global competitors can catch up with them very quickly.

c. Settlement and Delivery Risk This risk takes place on cash settlement day. It occurs when company *A* has already transferred certain goods (including financial certificates evidencing cash values) to company *B*, but company *B* has failed to settle in cash due to unexpected transactional events. For example, say company *A* sold 1,000 TV sets to company *B* at $1,000 per set. On settlement day (the day *B* agreed to pay *A*), *A* should have received $1,000,000 in cash.

But due to issues arising from *B*'s bank (technology or any types of breakdown), *A* did not get the cash. Thus, this is also known as delivery risk, especially applicable to certain global transactions.

4. *Legal and Political Risks*

These risks occur primarily because of the special nature of legal or political environments.

a. Country Legal System Risk In virtually any situation, every contract would signify that it will be executed or interpreted based on a certain country's laws. For example, almost every foreign mutual fund company's redemption policy details would refer to procedures following the laws of the country where the fund was registered. When investors are unfamiliar with the legal differences between their home countries and the foreign county, certain risks may come into play.

b. Political Policies Risk New government officials are elected literally every day around the world. When new officials' policy platforms differ from the old ones, investment conditions may change. For example, a certain politician may be running for office and advocates stern environmental protection. If such a politician has a high possibility of winning, the environmental protection equipment manufacturer's stocks would be bid up.

Conversely, certain manufacturers currently dumping significant pollutants into the air and water may need to incur substantial costs in "cleaning up their acts." These costs would impact their future profits and thus their stock prices.

In short, risk and return generally go hand in hand. Realistically, setting high return goals generally is tougher than quantifying associated risks. Yet we have to start somewhere.

Although risk management is essential in every investment, investors should also act accordingly after performing due diligence. Through my years of investing, I have found that doomsayers exist in every country, predicting that "the end of the world" is coming soon. Most of time, their predictions came with vague time frames; thus, they do not really help investors.

Such dire predictions could be kept fresh repeatedly into the future. Thus it is conceivable that one day those predictions might come true without generating any value for current investors.

D. Maxim No. 5: Manage and Accept Portfolio Risks

1. How Much Can You Lose?

1. Your financial targets may include buying a new car or a larger house or saving for a college education or retirement. You should allocate your resources based on the two recommended types of portfolios.

   An old traditional guideline is that your higher-risk portfolio (satellite) percentage should be equal to 100 minus your age. For example, if you are 30, the risk portion of your total portfolio (or satellite portfolio) might be as high as 70%. But if you are 60, then your satellite portfolio should be only 40%. I personally feel that this is too approximate for most investors, as it does not take into account family responsibilities and future aspirations. Thus I encourage each investor to decide based on his or her own personal situation.
2. When you decide to buy an investment target, rather than invest 100% of allocated money all at one time, you might consider buying in certain proportions—for example, 1/3, 1/3, and 1/3. Unless you are a major investor, you may be subjected to numerous hidden market forces that could affect your buying prices.

For a list of five highly simplified factors to review before making an investment, see Box 5.1.

Box 5.1: Highly Simplified Factors to Review Before Making Any Investment (CLEMM)

Before you purchase an asset, you may wish to review CLEMM so you can quickly tick off these five common risks (though intended not to be exhaustive) to see whether they violate your own guidelines.

C: Credit Risk

Is your investment target rated by credit agencies? If not, can you run a quick verification that it is a reasonable credit risk?

If you are a conservative investor, try to view risks comparable to investment grades. Referencing the S&P rating system, they would be equivalent to ratings BBB or above, such as A, AA, or AAA.

L: Liquidity Risk

If and when you wish to convert a chosen investment target to cash, is there a ready market? What is the trading volume now? Here I refer to the investor's own liquidity needs, and not so much the liquidity of the company selling you the asset.

Think cash convertibility. If you need to sell this asset urgently, are buyers readily available, even during adverse economic conditions?

E: Exit Risk

If and when you wish to exit this investment, are there any fees or costs or any conditions to exit?

Certain investment products would incur exit fees if they were sold prior to an agreed-on time period. For

(*continued*)

example, certain mutual fund managers claim that their funds have no sales front-load fees. However, there may be funds with a graduated exit fee structure such as:

- Sale within first year, exit fee of 4%
- If within second year, 3%
- If within third year, 2%
- If within fourth year, 1%
- After fourth year, none

M: Money Type Risk

Is this investment target denominated in the same currency as your future cash outflow? Is this target currency likely to depreciate or appreciate?

At the writing of this chapter (early 2012), an investment denominated in Chinese RMB currency is considered favorable, due to the additional expected appreciation benefit against many currencies. Conversely, when investments are denominated in a perceived weaker currency, the resultant return in the home currency may be reduced.

M: Maturity Risk (Reinvestment Risk)

At the time you plan to sell your target investment or at maturity date, are there any reinvestment risks in the new investment environment at that time?

This risk is especially applicable to fixed-income investments upon maturity. Even before maturity, current valuation is critical for long-dated instruments (say over seven years). If the time frame is so remote, predicting interest rates and other economic conditions becomes increasingly uncertain; thus, more caution is called for.

Although stocks are popular in many countries, numerous investment assets should also be considered in your overall portfolio. To realize fixed income, in addition to deposits in banks, other avenues are bonds or real estate.

Obviously, for investors with certain expertise, commodities, derivatives, and structured products might be considered.

I wish to caution investors not to be pressured into buying assets by aggressive sales managers. We all have heard anecdotes of friends who boldly purchased assets out of their leagues; they need to unfortunately fall back on the BHP (buy, hold, and pray) methodology. In conclusion, regarding any new, fashionable, and "sexy" investments, if you do decide to proceed, allocate them to your satellite portfolio with a maximum exposure of say 20% to 40% of your total portfolio.

Overall reminder on portfolio construction

1. Search for substantial over-performance.

   If history is a useful guide, most individual investors try to outperform the market substantially, but with miserable results. The desire to find the next winning stock, say with a compound growth of 50% every year is overwhelming. Often the over zealous desire to excel by purchasing the next winner overshadows the basic homework needed to stay with the fundamentals of the company or the industry.

As a reminder, let me call your attention to the power of compounding. Starting with the "7% rule," you may recall that even for 7% compound returns, your portfolio will double in 10 years. For 15% compounding, your portfolio will double in five years. For 25%, it will double in three years. For other compounding percentages, see Figure 5.3.

The important point here is stick to your own target time frame and investment selections. Often when the overall market seems to be going through difficult times, investors reduce their exposure to stocks. But that may be a time for maintaining one's position. In many cases investors get out of the market at the bottom and get in when the market has already reached the top.

That is why I emphasize that you know your selected industries well with respect to economic cycles and have the confidence to do the right thing. You will belong to a select, elite group of individual investors who can stand tall over other investors who succumb to the age-old typical behavioral mistake.

2. Stay with your own strength.

As discussed in Chapters 2 and 4, accumulate your knowledge and stay with your own

Figure 5.3 The Power of Compounding Profits

Increase/year		**7%**	**10%**	**15%**	**20%**	**25%**	**30%**	**40%**	**50%**
Start $		100	100	100	100	100	100	100	100
Year	1	107	110	115	120	125	130	140	150
Year	2	114	121	132	144	156	169	196	225
Year	3	123	133	152	173	195	220	274	338
Year	4	131	146	175	207	244	286	384	506
Year	5	140	161	201	249	305	371	538	759
Year	6	150	177	231	299	381	483	753	1,139
Year	7	161	195	266	358	477	627	1,054	1,709
Year	8	172	214	306	430	596	816	1,476	2,563
Year	9	184	236	352	516	745	1,060	2,066	3,844
Year	10	197	259	405	619	931	1,379	2,893	5,767

strength in chosen industries, and select those superior companies in your portfolio.

As highlighted in Chapter 3, it is easy to be sidetracked by the endless bombardment of new information from the media. Although most stock experts mean well, you still need to judge whether they are distractions to managing your portfolio. You should stay cool and use the information for reference only. You need to believe in your own judgment,

3. Be wary of "noise."

   Although some TV stock gurus can be truly helpful, you must learn to have the conviction to decide whether these gurus are making sense or are simply contributing to the noise in the market.

   The noise producers come in all formats. Common types include

   a. Someone who used to have fame and power
   b. Someone who has little experience in a certain industry or economic area, but pretends to be an expert
   c. Someone who just wishes to attract attention by making controversial predictions

4. Focus on real information.

   In order to benefit from information sources, sharpen your evaluation of a commentator's education, background, and experience as well as that person's intention in making certain comments. As you become critical, you will be able to focus on real information and to ignore personalities dishing out garbage information.

Try to develop your own reliable information sources and stay with them. You need quality information here, not quantity, to guide your portfolio construction.

You'll be amazed how many of us are prone to believe information given by personalities, simply because they appear on TV or their views are printed in financial and investment magazines and newspapers.

You must be vigilant in filtering out what is relevant and beneficial in building your portfolio, given the sheer information explosion around us.

5. Build your portfolio methodically.

   You may wish to start with 100% cash or other safe assets; you then build your portfolio methodically, adding one industry at a time.

   With each chosen industry (see Chapter 2), accumulate your chosen stocks strategically—that is, buy via three tranches: 34%, 33%, and 33%?

   Depending on the size and nature of your chosen industry, you would accumulate the top companies—say, three or at maximum five companies. Try to limit your maximum exposure per stock to 5% of your portfolio, and if you exceed 5%, that stock must indeed be very safe and can "walk on water."

When you feel that you have exhausted the investment opportunities in your first industry, you may begin to study a second. Once you have adopted it as your chosen industry, again accumulate over time the next three to five best stocks in that industry.

Then step by step, you build up your portfolio, one industry at a time, with a speed depending on how much time you can devote to tracking your chosen industries. Now as you add more industries to your portfolio, you are indeed diversifying meaningfully, instead of blindly as do many individual investors.

Meanwhile, be patient, stay in cash or other safe non stock investments. You have to preserve your liquidity for future brighter opportunities.

2. No Chips? No Play!

If we may borrow a saying from Las Vegas or Macau, this game is not unlike going to a casino. The basic theme of this section is that however you wish to play this investment game, you need to preserve your fighting resources.

When you show up at a casino table, if you do not have chips, you simply are not allowed to play, period. So you must plan your investment game well. Whether you gain or not at any given time, always remember to conserve your fighting power to ensure that you have some chips left to play in subsequent games.

Action Plan

1. Considering your own future needs, tempered by your risk tolerance, you should adjust your resources based on a core portfolio and a satellite portfolio. In other words, have a guideline and stick to it.
2. Think through investment risks, which can be broadly categorized into market risks, credit risks, operating risks, and legal or political risks. Only after you have processed these risks should you invest your hard-earned money.
3. When investing in stocks or other assets (e.g., bonds, structured notes), you should focus on pertinent major aspects. You may refer to "CLEMM" in Box 5.1 for a quick reminder list of applicable risks.
4. Remember: No Chips? No Play!

Chapter 6

Capitalize on Policy Directions

Are Policies Your Friends?

Regardless of how you feel about the fairness of new policies, you should capitalize on investment trends emerging from evolving policies.

A. Are Policies Fair?

Regardless of whether you feel the situations are fair or not for investment purposes, I recommend you not to fight the politicians' policies or intentions.

We often react to new policies from politicians or regulators in terms of whether they are right or fair. However, in the investment world there should be no emotions. In fact, once you feel that you could capitalize on any special situations arising from a new policy, you may wish to immediately adjust your investment strategies or tactics, based on these new trends. Try also to assess the relative stability of the policies with respect to your portfolio objectives.

Once you have done this, if you still wish to take other non investment actions that reflect your emotions as to fair or not fair, proceed to do so by all means.

B. Policy Directions

Because investments and policies are so closely related, I would like to set forth the following reminders to be incorporated into your portfolio strategies.

1. Trade Policy

You should benefit from trade policies not just from those of your own country but of countries around the world.

For example, focusing on the Middle East, if a situation similar to the 1973 OPEC oil embargo arises, you may wish to prepare yourself as to how to adjust your strategies in your portfolio, especially for stocks directly related to energy.

In Hong Kong, when Closer Economic Partnership Arrangements (CEPA) was formulated to begin in 2004 between Hong Kong and the Chinese mainland, people debated the pros and cons of its effects. In addition, many opinions were that these policies might affect their own personal situations or businesses, positively or negatively. Instead of spending a lot of time debating these policies, an opportune investor would immediately take advantage of the future trends based on their effects on trade, infrastructure, employment, and so forth.

2. *Fiscal Policy*

Here is another example. Regulators' policies on quantitative easing (QE1 and QE2) have been implemented in the United States, designed to stimulate the economy following the 2008–2009 crisis. Remember, a government has virtually unlimited resources to influence banks and numerous government agencies, at least as compared with the resources of traditional investors or corporations.

As QEs were implemented, U.S. interest rates were effectively "controlled" as planned. As numerous bonds were purchased from the banks, bond values predictably increased. This effect of pushing down bond rates eventually influenced the lending rates between banks (the far reaching interbank interest rates) throughout all the financial markets.

As interest rates were moving in the zero direction, borrowing costs for all private sectors were significantly reduced as well. This move was expected to stimulate investment and pull the economy out of its doldrums.

Many economists commented that the QE2 has positively affected the stock market, which in turn contributed to increasing consumption and a better economy. However, the desirability of QE1 and QE2 was questioned by many academicians and politicians. Quantitative easing might cause higher inflation if the amounts of the QEs were not properly calibrated.

As mentioned, although one can debate these monetary policies for many years, stock markets are reacting swiftly even though these debates may go on for years. Thus, investors need to adjust their portfolio asset allocations and other strategies, inasmuch as many institutions are flush with liquidity.

Except for some minor corrections, the stock market performed well during QE1 and QE2. As this unusual liquidity flooded the stock market, most of the indices did well, coupled with certain selected improvements in the U.S. economic indicators.

Given the expansion of the U.S. balance sheet, many investment gurus are predicting the possibility of the downfall of the U.S. dollar and subsequent inflation. How soon this will happen would depend on future U.S. fiscal policies along with numerous global factors (e.g., the emerging debt issues with a number of European countries). In any case, investors should be reminded to factor in global fiscal policies in their portfolio asset allocation.

3. Political Elections and Policies

We all understand that elected officials have various impacts on investments for different countries; therefore, an astute investor should look for certain behavioral trends.

Presidential Elections Whenever there are election cycles, politicians will promote policies to favor their platforms or any economic policies they wish to convince their constituents or the general public. This "election factor" is quite common in many countries. I wish to remind you of a strong correlation between an economy and the respective country's political leadership term and time frame.

In October 2010, the U.S. government announced that the QE2 (quantitative easing—phase 2) would be needed to continue to stimulate the economy. According to some political observers, this would help the incumbent party in mid-term elections. With this and other related government programs, many investors anticipated that they would provide a positive impetus for the economy. The stock market reacted positively, and the S&P 500 Index advanced approximately 10.8% from October 27, 2010 to March 25, 2011, despite an economy that had many issues.

You may or may not feel that the QE2 was wise or effective. But if you happen to trade the market, you could benefit accordingly. Remember, you may not agree with the correctness of the policies, optimal investment strategies should not be affected by one's emotions.

For example, in September 2011 "Operation Twist" was started as an attempt to stimulate the U.S. economy. By driving down the long-term rates, this move would reduce the cost of borrowing for consumers and money-strapped institutions. However, due to many external worrisome financial factors at the time, stock markets throughout the world (including in the United States) appeared not to have benefited from such policies, at least not significantly.

As investors analyzed and debated the desirability of "Operation Twist," the stock markets reacted accordingly.

Key Point

Wise investors would have already quickly accounted for political leaders' policies in their portfolio strategies.

Apparent Correlation of Stock Price with Political Presidential Term In many countries, the stock market often shows a strong correlation with the country's presidential term and time frame. For example, the United States has a four-year presidential election system. Many studies show that the stock market statistics appear to have correlations with certain timelines of the presidential term by years.

The third year of the U.S. presidential cycle has been historically ebullient for stocks, with an average increase of around 19%.

Note on More Detailed Statistics Beginning in 1925, tracking the U.S. presidential four-year terms through 2010, the S&P 500 Index approximates that average performances were, respectively, +8% the first year, +9% the second year, +19% the third year, and +11% the fourth year.

Since 1939, no negative return has been recorded in the third year of a presidential term on the basis of the S&P 500. The range of positive returns varies widely over the third years. Positive returns varied approximately from 5% in 1947 to 38% in 1995.

Obviously, one never can tell whether this correlation would continue. However, this is additional evidence of how a stock market can be influenced by political events. You may wish to study similar evidence in your own country in managing your portfolios.

Going back to the U.S. presidential "third year" phenomenon, I would caution you not to blindly follow any correlation statistics without using your own judgment. Numerous global events could easily distort such a historical correlation.

C. Maxim No. 6: Profit from Policies and Trends

1. Anticipate Policies

You may disagree with certain government policymakers' policies (e.g., the federal government's recent policies in saving Bank of America, Citibank, and AIG, etc.). Many negative opinions were to the effect that if the government were to continue to leverage its balance sheet, many generations might be affected in the future. While many people would spend time arguing over these policies, you should be the one thinking about how to anticipate the trend and benefit from it.

In short, I highly recommended that you think along with the government and foresee what might happen and act appropriately. Obviously, you may need to exercise your judgment on overly zealous promises made by politicians to further their own elections.

2. Don't Fight, Join

In case you do not have time to anticipate new policies, at least try to stay cool when policies are implemented. Don't fight them; join and benefit from the trends, at least from an investment standpoint.

Action Plan

1. Regardless of your portfolio strategies, do not fight regulatory actions and policies.
2. Better yet, think along closely with regulators if possible. Be well informed on their possible actions, long before their policies are actually implemented.
3. Recognize that political changes are the reality in any country and welcome them. Luck comes to you if you pay attention and are ready.

Chapter 7

Loving an Investment or Loving to Make Money

Falling in Love

Loving an investment and loving to profit from investments are totally different things.

A. Is "Love" Forever?

Don't fall in love with any investment. Of course, I generally encourage you to fall in love with your special "someone," but I certainly would not advise you to fall in love with any investment.

Tech Crash of 2000–2001

I am sure you recall the tech crash of 2000–2001. I recall the case of Paul, a Canadian architect, age 60 at the time. He was doing very well buying technological stocks in 1998–1999. He was doing so well that he had plans to travel around the world and move to a million-dollar house.

He wanted to make a killing because of the constantly rising prices of tech stocks. He bought technological stocks exclusively, because he had repeatedly made money with these stocks, so much that he fell in love with them. He sold all his other stocks and investments and moved practically all his retirement money into tech stocks, especially into speculative high-risk companies. Then the crash came. His portfolio value went down 80% before he sold out.

Basically he lost most of his retirement money. Now Paul has to work again. Due to his frail health and age, now over 70, he could not find a permanent position. Very sad. The last time I heard from a friend, he was doing part-time work, selling hamburgers at a fast food store to supplement the income from his remaining financial resources. Sad, but true!

No Emotions

In any investment, therefore, you must stay cool—no emotions. Regardless of how "perfect" you think a stock might be, you need to follow the market prices regularly, as much as your time allows. The economy will go up or down, being affected by many conditions. As a good investor, you need to discipline yourself and understand that all stocks are subject to laws of supply and demand. You need to be aware of consumer sentiments and market factors.

B. All-or-Nothing Thinking

I also wish to caution you about an all-or-nothing strategy, which could be dangerous, even though it may make for great stories that you can tell at cocktail parties when you win.

Key Point

Realize that truly successful investors who are guided by this type of thinking are very rare indeed.

I am reminded also of Jenny, a doctor of alternative medicine, who is very smart and well educated, medically speaking. However, her broker friend recommended that she invest in commodity futures, such as oil futures. In the beginning, Jenny was happy, as she was making good money from her contracts. However, her broker friend never told her about the huge risks involved, although she had already fallen in love with commodity futures very quickly. Her profits even dwarfed her regular income as a doctor.

Then the tide turned. Her positions now were losing money, and her broker asked her for more collateral money. Since she was in love with her commodity futures, she was not willing to let go. After exhausting her savings, she asked her brothers and sisters for more money; her broker friend was guessing the price would turn around anytime soon. It never happened. Now Jenny approached her father and mother for more money, but still the prices kept going down.

She refused to admit her mistake and get out. She then got loans from underground unlicensed lenders.

To make a long story short, she finally had to declare bankruptcy herself. Meanwhile, she had damaged the financial health of everybody around her. For a while, before she cleared all her loans, she was fearful of her physical safety.

C. Love a Person? Invest for Love?

Given that we are all human, we often invest based on loving a person and investing due to the love relationship. In other words, we may unconsciously make an investment decision based on our existing good feeling for or love of a person without doing due diligence.

Being human, it is natural for us to have emotional ties to the people around us.

Through my investment years, I recall many investors who would simplify their homework or make a deliberate quick judgment due to their being totally mired in strong emotions.

I've also seen friends in responsible high positions doing methodical and meaningful investment analyses on normal transactions. But once relationships crept in, their good judgment just crumbled. Manifestations of love or good feeling include

1. Love between relatives (parents, sons and daughters, other relatives)
2. Love between spouses (or lovers)
3. Friendship (old classmates, social friends)
4. Coworkers (business friends)

Key Point

We often fear that the quality of a relationship may diminish if we do not proceed with a certain investment, as the prime purpose of that investment is to please the person we love. This thinking is historically a recipe for disaster. Remember: Make investments based solely on their own merit.

Several years ago, Felix was in the import/export business and ran a successful and profitable company. He had accumulated some wealth personally. Felix had a lovely wife (Janet) and loved her very much. According to Janet, she was approached by a high-profile international investment company that specialized in high-return investments.

The company's minimum investment threshold started at $500,000. Janet liked this company very much because its directors promoted very high-return investment products, including one with an expected 100% return in six months.

Though Felix wanted to proceed according to Janet's wishes, he felt a little uneasy due to the nature of the product and its return. Felix knew that I had been in banking and investment for many years. He urged me to sit in on the final presentation from the company's president before handing over his $500,000 check. Originally, I had zero interest in these "high-return" presentations, as I had sat through too many similar meetings during my career, but Felix was insistent and I finally agreed.

The presentation was planned to take place in an imposing conference room in a high-class financial building. The company organized presentations by five senior executives including its president. They were all tall and good looking and well dressed in immaculate, expensive suits. Their aura gave me an unmistakable image of global, successful bankers.

Before making the actual presentation, they were introduced as graduates of famous universities who had worked at large international banks for over 20 years. We were impressed by their credentials, and they presented their product: trading banking guarantees. I was somewhat familiar with trading bank guarantees and was aware that they could indeed potentially yield high returns for successful traders.

There are many types of bank guarantee (BG). One of the common types is for credit transactions; in a normal buy–sell transaction, a buyer would use a BG in favor of the seller-beneficiary on settlement date under certain terms. Thus a BG could be viewed as an insurance function for the beneficiary at a future time frame.

Before the BG's expiration date it could be traded among possible investors. New owners would purchase these BGs at face value with discount. BG traders would trade BGs, earning spreads on various discounts, often over short time intervals.

However, in this case, the presenters openly told us not to seek professional opinions from regular financial consultants, as many deals are confided only to potential investors on a need-to-know basis. Moreover, the presenters also warned us not share their details with anyone, as these were secrets. If too many people know about them, the investment return might be "watered down."

After the hour-long presentation, both Janet and Felix agreed that this was absolutely a "once in a life time opportunity." To boost the sales probability, the company had also invited Janet's neighbor friend (Joyce) to join, as Joyce had also agreed to invest in this "winner."

To make a long story short, after the dramatic presentations I suggested to Felix that he hold his check, as I had numerous issues with the sales pitches. Now Felix was not happy, because Janet wanted to get this done that day. Both felt that I was blocking them from an opportunity to make huge profits.

Frankly speaking, I have sat through these must-win presentations many times. I therefore could truly listen in a super-calm manner and thus remain immune to the super claims.

I told Felix that this was a scam, even though the presentations were super-packaged. Although the presenters employed proper banking terminology and had memorized key facts, they were totally flabbergasted when I started to ask them about strategic pricing and settlement details.

I sort of felt sorry for these five good-looking bankers, as I had ruined their chance of conning a potential investor. When I finally had time to explain to Felix, he was in tears, knowing that he meant to please his lovely wife. He had become too emotional and had not done any due diligence.

D. Maxim No. 7: Emotions and Investment Don't Mix

1. Review and Learn

Review your existing investments honestly. Try to objectively judge whether you have any emotions or "attachments" to them as a result of some past experience. Recognize the weakness of human nature. It is human nature to resist admitting mistakes.

Historically, great investors are not heroes or heroines, at least not every time. Truly wise investors never "fall in love" with their investments.

2. No Love, Just Make Money

Don't fall in love; just make money, one target at a time. Learn and know a stock as much as you can for future decisions, but don't fall in love. You'll find this new thinking practical. Be mindful of your decisions when relationship elements are present, either due to loving someone or for any family or friendship reasons. This approach will free you from past bondage and make you a more successful investor.

Action Plan

1. Use discipline in your investments while holding your emotions in check. Regardless of how "perfect" an investment may be or may have been, don't fall in love with it.
2. The goal of investment is to seek a material return. Return on investment should be your primary measurement.
3. If one adds "feelings" to an investment, decision and judgment can be clouded unconsciously, creating many idiots historically. So once you sense an emotional feeling associated with an investment, you must heed the warning signals.

Chapter 8

Fully Enjoy Your Profits from Stocks

Rich and Healthy or Rich with Pain

Treat investment as a way of life, not merely as a separate project.

A. Manage Your Investment Lifestyle and Health Simultaneously

Investment should not be a stop-and-go activity. A good analogy would be going on a diet. Presumably, a good diet should not be simply a fad. A good investment style should be ongoing as a way of life if it is to be truly successful over the long term. If you have ever embarked on a diet, you can draw your own conclusions, whether you wish your results to be long term or just short term.

Most effective diets have been promoted as being a change in a person's lifestyle, not just a project. This applies also to investments.

B. Swap Poor Health for Big Money

You can exchange poor health for good investment results. I have known friends who have been successful in investments from time to time. But to achieve those investment gains, they suffer from poor appetite and sleepless nights, even ruining their health permanently in the process.

Let us examine some individuals' lifestyles as they are affected by their stock investments. Most investors are so overpowered by their need to know the latest developments in the investment world that they are constantly anxious about missing the latest news. Thus, every day in the week (including weekends) and throughout the day (including meal times) they nervously rush to learn the latest from their TVs or eagerly pump their friends for the most recent investment news.

This is no way to live a balanced life. Yes, investment is important in that additional profits from stocks could enhance our lifestyles. But my humble opinion is that people should have life beyond investments.

As you follow the advice contained in the previous seven chapters, I encourage you to develop your own investment thinking style and form a proper investment habit. For example, as discussed in Chapter 2, once you have identified your chosen industry—or a few industries—as your targets, you do not have to be anxious about missing some news about industries that are totally unrelated to yours.

For instance, if certain oil exporting countries decide to cut back production or increase crude oil prices, certainly airline stocks would be affected, given that fuel oil represents a major airline operating cost. But if your chosen industry is luxury goods retailers (as with Mary in Chapter 2), you should not care too much, as the effect on your portfolio would be small, if any—at least not directly.

But if your portfolio is spread out all over the 100 industries and/or sectors, you would try to capture everything in the news, because almost any news may affect your portfolio!

Key Point

Stay focused on a few industries, and live a more relaxed life.

Therefore, I propose that investment activity should be a way of life and should not damage your health. If you follow this book methodically, you will succeed while having the good health to enjoy your money. Organ transplants can be expensive, not to talk about the pain and suffering that goes with the operations.

I advocate that you learn the basic concepts explained in this book, step by step, and work toward your successful financial future. If you follow the advice in this book, you will get effective results, as the validity of these concepts has been proven over the past 20 years.

C. Investment Emotions That Are Detrimental to Our Health

Among the many extreme emotions that could ruin our health, I would highlight the three most common emotions to avoid or at least to minimize as much as possible: worry, fear, and anger.

1. Worry

According to historical statistics, most average investors feel that they can pick stocks based on their own ability. As pointed out in previous chapters, individual investors are playing these stock games not just among themselves, but against other big investors, with stock prices being subject to their powerful influence on supply and demand.

When individual investors realize that they are losing control when expected price gains do not happen, they worry. Their confidence is shaken, and they don't know what to do.

Potential losses are affecting their mood and may affect their appetite and sleep. Many would comfort themselves by pretending to be optimistic, but that is fairly useless in the real jungle of investments. Worry and sheer hoping just do not help in making and tracking investments—sad, but true.

This reminds me of Jonathan (an excellent high school teacher) who read investment reports that made new recommendations on a gold-mining company. He was in his own world, extrapolating past performances of this high-flying stock, not taking the time to understand the company or the mining industry basics. He never took time to learn the criteria of success applicable to these investments. Yet he decided to invest in this one stock and prepared to make a killing with most of his savings.

Jonathan began to worry when the stock price dropped below his cost and "prayed" that the investment would one day turn around. He started to develop a stomach ulcer, experiencing severe pains almost every day. He drank excessively, trying to drown that "down" feeling. His health began to deteriorate.

2. Fear

As the "paper loss" got larger, Jonathan's fear began to sink in. When that emotion struck, he suddenly was gripped by intense fear and began thinking illogically. Now he interpreted all new information in a pessimistic manner. even when such information might probably have helped him to act professionally. His drinking got worse, and his liver also suffered due to over-consumption of alcohol on daily basis.

He started losing his own confidence and his ability to think and analyze facts clearly. Meanwhile, his stomach ulcer and liver conditions continued to worsen as stress built up even more.

3. Anger

Jonathan's fear soon turned into anger. He tried to get even with the market. He was advised by a "friendly" stock expert to buy more to average down his costs. He kept buying more as prices went down further, not spending the time to find out why the stock price kept falling.

As Jonathan's losses got even bigger, his fear and anger kept on feeding each other. Meanwhile, his health deteriorated to the point that he could not even function normally at his own regular teaching work. When he could not bear the pressure anymore, he finally capitulated; he sold all his positions and realized a huge loss.

Unfortunately, his stomach and liver conditions were so bad that he never recovered his health. Yet he probably never learned, like many individual investors who make similar mistakes again and again.

In retrospect, Jonathan should have learned that this mining company was overleveraged in its balance sheet to begin with. Along with speculative and poor senior management, the company had cash flow problems in meeting debt obligations. The potential profit never happened, as once speculated by unsubstantiated industry gurus. If Jonathan had done even minimal homework, he would not have gone crazy with this investment target by "betting his farm," and his health would not have been damaged permanently.

D. Investment Flowchart

To enjoy an investment process and the associated profits, I recommend that you examine the flowchart shown in Figure 8.1 and refer back to the related chapters.

Figure 8.1 Investment Flowchart

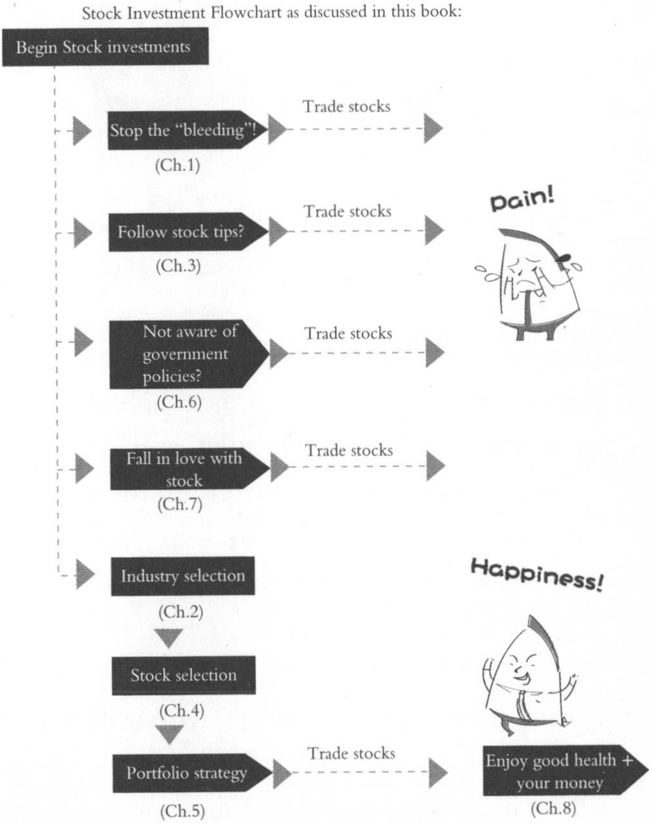

Stock Investment Flowchart as discussed in this book:

Begin Stock investments

Stop the "bleeding"! (Ch.1) → Trade stocks →

Follow stock tips? (Ch.3) → Trade stocks →

Not aware of government policies? (Ch.6) → Trade stocks →

Fall in love with stock (Ch.7) → Trade stocks →

Pain!

Industry selection (Ch.2)

Stock selection (Ch.4)

Portfolio strategy (Ch.5) → Trade stocks → Enjoy good health + your money (Ch.8)

Happiness!

E. Maxim No. 8: Maintain Health and Wealth

1. Sleep well, take care of your health, and follow the suggestions in this book.

(Remember, if your investments are well structured, they increase in value even when you sleep.)

2. Even if you follow all the concepts in this book, your success would not be necessarily a straight line. Like life itself, you will have wins and losses, and you learn from them every time. Predictably and step by step, you'll have more systematic wins than occasional losses, and you'll be on your way to riches.
3. What good is your money if you cannot enjoy it with good health? Worst yet, with millions to your name, you may live a long life but live it sitting in a wheelchair with tubes connected all over you.

Action Plan

1. Enjoy your money with good health and not in a wheelchair.
2. Be patient, be disciplined, and you will win.
3. Others have done so using my maxims, so can you.

Appendix A

Basic Technical Analysis

In addition to fundamental analysis (marketing, financial, operating indicators, etc.), technical analysis (TA) can be used to assist in predicting future stock prices. An investor who has working knowledge of both types of analysis can certainly be more effective in deciding buy–sell prices.

Because many TA books are available for purchase, I won't go into details here. I would encourage my readers to access these books to acquire a working knowledge of TA principles. Still, I feel the reader should be familiar with the most basic tools, as discussed in the following text.

Note: For readers who happen to be TA gurus, I need to grossly simplify the following discussion for the benefit of many readers new to TA. For this I apologize.

Although many styles of charting prevail, most popular charts can be categorized into three types, depending on the country in which you live. These three types are line, bar, and candlestick.

Learning TA can be a full-time job, and many books on the subject are 400 to 500 pages long. For super simplicity, let us philosophically categorize technical indicators into the three following types, as certain overlapping elements may exist:

1. Trend indicators
2. Market strength indicators
3. Variability and momentum indicators

Let us highlight some common TA indicators.

A. Trend Indicators

1. Exponential moving average (EMA)
   a. Short term (5 to 10 days)
   b. Medium term (20 to 30 to 50 days)
   c. Long term (100 to 200 days)

2. MACD line (moving average convergence/divergence)

   The purpose of this indicator is to measure and show the difference between two moving averages. For example, many TA practitioners like to compare the 30-day moving average with the 10-day moving average.

3. Oscillator line

   The more widely used oscillators are centered oscillators, also called by other names, such as internal strength indicators. Among other uses, they assist in determining relative trend strength in the future. The principle here is to use the values of two extreme points and discover short-term over bought or over sold conditions, thereby generating certain trend signals.

   When the oscillator line approaches the upper limit, the asset is deemed to be overbought. Alternatively, for lower-limit approaches, the asset is deemed to be over sold.

B. Strength Indicators

1. Volume

   This is simply the number of stock shares traded during a specific time period (e.g., day, week, month, etc.). One common concept is that a condition of rising prices together with increasing volume is considered bullish.

2. Volume oscillator

This indicator displays the difference between two moving averages of a stock's volume. This difference between the two moving averages may be expressed in percentages or other measurements. The difference between two moving averages of volume can be used to determine whether the overall volume trend is increasing or decreasing.

C. Variability and Momentum Indicators

1. Bollinger Bands (BB)

BB is a multifunctional tool, combining moving averages and standard deviation and is one of the more widely used TA tools. BB can be viewed as having the following three components:

a. Moving average: generally speaking, the 20-day moving average is popular.
b. Upper limit: generally, prices above the two standard deviations are popular, calculated using the 20-day moving average of closing prices.
c. Lower limit: generally, prices below the two standard deviations are popular, again calculated using the 20-day moving average of closing prices.

2. Stochastic indicator (SI)

   The SI may be viewed as a momentum type of indicator, showing within a certain cycle whether the stock price is at a lower or higher level. SI displays the relative speed of stock price movements, using the momentum change to assess price movements.

■ ■ ■

In short, using a combination of TA tools, one may gauge whether the stock is at a bullish or a bearish mode. Such information is helpful in developing timing strategies on expected stock price movements.

Let me here reiterate my recommendation not to rely on TA alone for buy–sell strategies. Fundamental analysis information should be used to back up one's own buy–sell decisions.

Appendix B

Deciding on Buy Prices

Let me now reemphasize that investors must assess their own personal situations and decide on their own risk acceptance levels and investment horizons. Stocks are risky by nature; investors must consider their age, family situation, cash flow needs, and the like and invest accordingly. The discussions that follow are for reference only.

For example, when you decide to invest a sum of money (100%), you may consider buying in via three tranches, the first at 34%, the second at 33%, and the third at 33%. In other words, if you have $10,000 to invest, the tranches would be in amounts of $3,400, $3,300, and $3,300, respectively.

Let us assume that after performing fundamental analysis, you select a stock and a "fair value" would be $72/share; thus you intend to buy at $72 or lower. For this example, large price fluctuations are purposely used to illustrate this "separate tranches" concept.

Referencing Figure B.1, you may wish to use technical analysis (TA) to determine your buy-in prices. If prices fall below the 20 MA line (20-day moving average) say in June, you may allocate $3,400 to buy at $70/share for 48.57 shares.

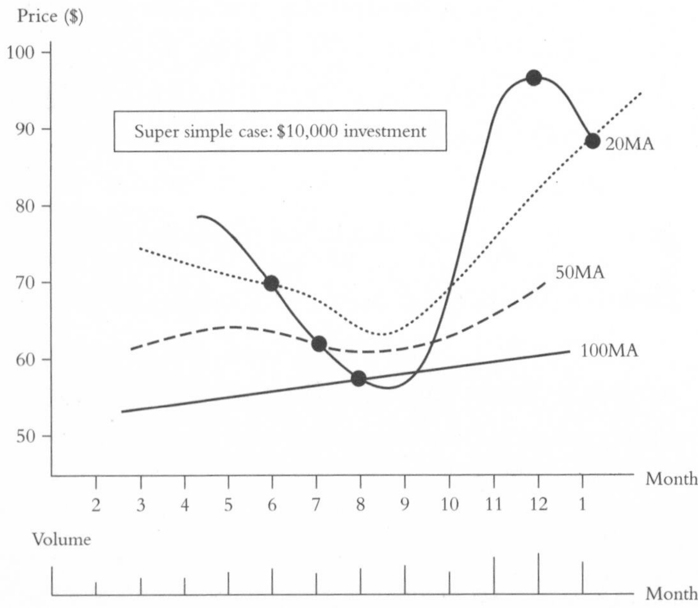

Figure B.2 Buy Using Several Tranches to Lower Your Costs

	Amount ($)	Indicator	Time	Price/ Share ($)	Number of Shares
	3,400	20 MA	June	70	48.57
Buy	3,300	50 MA	July	62	53.22
	3,300	100 MA	August	57	57.89
Total	10,000				

Assuming the price continues to drop in July and hits the 50 MA line, you may use $3,300 to buy more at $62/share for 53.22 shares.

Figure B.2 shows a really simple example of a $10,000 investment.

Assuming further that the price continues to fall in August and hits the 100 MA line, you can then use the remaining $3,300 to buy at $57/share for 57.89 shares. (Please refer to the summary table in Figure B.2.)

If you were able to buy in for all three tranches, you would now accumulate 159.68 shares:

- At $70/share, for $3,400, you bought 48.57 shares.
- At $62/share, for $3,300, you bought 53.22 shares.
- At $57/share, for $3,300, you bought 57.89 shares.

The total accumulated position is 159.68 shares.

Case Results

1. If the market price in December rises to $100, your asset value would be $15,968, or +59.6% profit.
2. If the market price in January falls to $90, your asset value would be $14,372 or +43.7% profit.

When comparing your fair value buy-in price of $72 using the whole $10,000 amount at one time, this accumulated position would have 138.88 shares only. Thus this three-tranche methodology would increase your holding of total shares by 20.81 shares (159.68 − 138.88 = 20.8), using Case Result #1 as an example.

Obviously, this is a fictitious example to illustrate the multi-tranche methodology. The price fluctuations were purposely enlarged to illustrate the benefits; in reality, price fluctuations may be smaller.

Now let us assume the price in July falls only below the 50 MA line but not the 100 MA line. In this case, you would have accumulated only 101.79 shares (48.57 + 53.22 shares). Given this situation, you would just have to be patient and wait. Remember, due to the nature of the stock market, you could never know all the everyday factors affecting a stock price.

Having said that, as you continue to track the stock using fundamental analysis, you may discover that the company may have additional superior features not previously accounted for.

In such a case, you may wish to adjust your buy-in price for your third tranche. That is, you would consider using the 50 MA line as your "fair buy-in price" as well. Market conditions change, and therefore tracking using fundamental analysis is critical to determine your buy-in price.

To reiterate: to be successful in making money in the stock market, you must choose an industry (see Chapter 2) and select a few top companies that you feel comfortable with.

You would probably know as much as traditional stock analysts (if not more), because you have the luxury of concentrating your homework on these few chosen companies over a long period of time, whereas the analysts may need to cover numerous stocks for numerous industries, following directives from their institutional bosses.

You do not need to buy 100 stocks to make big money. Time has proven that you can make big money, again and again, by choosing just a few superior stocks.

When you have developed expertise on one industry, I recommend that you diversify by focusing on another industry, adding one industry at a time, always under your control.

Using the P/E ratio (stock price/earnings per share) is a popular way to gauge whether a stock is over-bought or over-sold. For each industry, the market appears to agree with the standard views on the range of P/E, rightly or wrongly. (You may also use P/E for reference, although I would humbly rate price/cash flow per share [P/CF] as a better measure.)

In any case, if the historical P/E range of a stock is between 8 and 35, buying at P/Es close to 35 (say 32) would be high risk, unless your fundamental analysis justifies such an action. On the contrary, if you can buy in at the low range (say 11), risks may be lower; again, this must be confirmed through fundamental analysis.

Using P/E alone to judge a stock is dangerous; other financial analysis should be used to confirm buy-in prices.

Appendix C

Deciding on Sell Prices

After you have followed Chapters 2, 3, 4 and selected your stocks, you may continue to hold your stocks and enjoy your "paper profits." But in these volatile times, even the best stocks have their volatility.

As discussed in previous chapters, after doing proper homework, you will have a better appreciation of a stock's intrinsic value. When market prices exceed the intrinsic values, you may wish to cash out and realize the fruits of your labor.

In order to protect your original principal and conserve your future "investment bullets," you may wish to put "cash out" mechanisms in place. Since investors have various investment goals and risk considerations, I propose the following three "sell price" methodologies for your consideration.

A. Preset Sell Price Based on Percentage of Original Price

This methodology is the simplest of all, in that it involves the least amount of thought and setup time. If you are a shorter-term investor, you may decide on a sell price based on, say, a 5% variation. For example, for a $100 original price, your sell price would be either $105 or $95. Obviously, you will be pleased if you gain $5 or 5%. Some short-term investors prefer this methodology, as by gaining 5%, say, for even 10 times a year, the return on investment (simple calculation basis) would be 50%, nothing to be sneezed at.

On the other hand, in case you sell out at $95, a loss of 5%, you would be unhappy. However, it is not the end of the world as you still have $95 as an investment base for future investments, also nothing to be sneezed at, as your stop loss is working to conserve your principal.

B. Set Up a Moving Percentage Sell Price

This methodology involves a sliding percentage calculation based on the most recent highest prices.

1. For example, for an original buy price of $100, using a 5% sell limit trigger, one would sell when market price reaches $95.
2. But if the market price increases to $105, using the same 5% trigger, the new sell limit would now be reset at $99.75 ($105 × 0.95).
3. If market price continues to climb to $110, then the new sell limit would also be increased to $104.5 ($110 × 0.95).
4. One major advantage of this methodology is that it protects your capital initially (here 5%) and captures previously increased price levels.

C. Use Technical Analysis (TA) Tools to Assist Sell Price Decisions

In addition to fundamental analysis, you may wish to use technical analysis (TA) tools as discussed in Appendix A. As mentioned, many TA tools exist, and tons of materials have already been published about them. As you become more familiar with the TA tools, you will gain insight into literally hundreds of tools, variations, and terms.

TA can truly be a "profession" in itself, employing descriptive terms to make investment homework lively. For example,

- A death cross, as a weak signal when a shorter MA line crosses a longer MA line from above
- A golden cross, as a strong signal when a shorter MA line crosses a longer MA line from below

(*Note*: MA = moving average.)

If you happen to like candlestick charts, you'll learn the benefits of reading a candlestick, with the "body" providing opening and closing prices and the "shadow" lines indicating highest and lowest trading prices for that time period.

Descriptive names also signal how the stock is doing. For example,

- A "shooting star" (i.e., when a candlestick has a small body, a long upper shadow, and little or no lower shadow); this pattern suggests a small reversal after a rally.
- A "hanging man" (i.e., a small body, and near a relatively high level, with a long lower shadow and little or no upper shadow); this pattern is considered bearish, especially if it happens after a big uptrend.

Life is never dull when you have investment friends who swear by the reliability of TA.

As a suggestion to begin, you may use moving average lines and Bollinger Band limits as sell warning signals, assuming you bought in at a relatively low price. Depending on the stock's volatility and your fundamental analysis, you might consider selling when increasing prices hit the 20-day moving average line (MA 20) or the upper limit line of the Bollinger Band, depending again on your investment horizon.

As you become an expert in your chosen industry and certain selected stocks, you will gain experience in their related price behaviors as an additional weapon in your arsenal.

Appendix D

Strategy for Investing in High-Dividend (HD) Stocks

Many books have been written about the pros and cons of investing in high-dividend (HD) stocks. To cover this entire area would be beyond the scope of this book. However, I would highlight certain key concepts that may be helpful in incorporating these stocks in your portfolio.

A. Who Should Consider This Strategy?

For certain classes of passive investors (e.g., retirees, some housewives, or busy workers who put in many hours of overtime), HD stocks should be considered.

B. Inclusion as HD Stocks

First of all, the definition of HD stocks varies, depending on which gurus you follow. In this Appendix, let us set a range of 2.5% to 10% yield return, thus covering many categories of high-dividend stocks. Obviously, risk and reward generally go together, and I caution my readers accordingly.

C. Basic Indicators for Choosing HD Stocks

Without going into fancy mathematics and difficult terminology, I would suggest looking at four indicators in selecting these companies. At minimum they should have

1. A relatively strong financial condition
2. Earnings stability and growth

3. A reasonable dividend payout ratio
4. A consistent history of dividends *and* dividend growth

D. Strategy Goal

The goal should be to generate a consistent stream of cash from aggregating dividends from a portfolio of stocks of relatively low-risk companies that have a track record of distributing reliable and growing dividends. This strategy is especially beneficial when cash flows from fixed-income instruments are inadequate because of a low-interest environment.

E. Company Selection Criteria

The following criteria should serve as a guide for choosing companies to invest in:

- The company has an understandable and sustainable business model, with a meaningful competitive edge (or moat).
- The company has a relatively strong financial condition as discussed in Chapter 4 (e.g., relatively low debt as compared with competitors in the same industry).
- Earnings stability is valued over high growth. Still, a reasonable earnings growth history as compared with other competitors in the

industry is certainly important. Pay attention to the nature of earnings (e.g., positive cash flow from core operations has a higher quality than simply accounting income).

- The company's growth should not be constrained by a high payout ratio relative to that industry. For example, if the dividend payout consistently usurps the bulk of the positive cash flow from core operations, the company's future growth plans may be compromised by such concerns as necessary capital expenditures for future expansion. For a normal business operation, generally speaking, a payout ratio exceeding 75% should be examined. Again, please compare the company with its peers in the same sector or industry to gauge the degree of appropriate payout percentage. For instance, in the U.S. mortgage REIT sector, a 90% return (or more) is common due to U.S. tax regulations.
- The company should have a consistent dividend record and steady dividend growth. Again, depending on the industry, a dividend growth of 3% or more a year is highly valued, at least during the past five years.

One should note, depending on the preference of the investor and his or her respective risk profile, that dividend growth rate is often more important than the absolute dividend yield rate for the current year.

F. Become Familiar with an HD Industry

I would reemphasize that you must learn the chosen industry or sector before plunking down your hard-earned money, as discussed in Chapter 2. You may wish to look into certain historically HD industries or sectors rather than traditional common stocks. It is essential to understand respective risks before you invest. Here are some HD areas to investigate:

- General common stocks of industrial/service companies
- Mortgage real estate investment trusts (REITs)
- Operating real estate REITs
- Business development companies (BDCs)
- Energy-related limited partnerships (LPs)

You may start your initial research by visiting any web site and then typing in specific sector or industry categories.

In short, this HD strategy is not for everyone, as it may not reach one's investment goals regarding price appreciation potential. Depending on the investor's needs, however, HD stocks should have an appropriate allocation in a portfolio, which would assist the investor to get a good night's sleep.

About the Author

Professor Philip Shu-Ying Cheng was the Chief Investment Officer at MetLife Taiwan, a wholly owned subsidiary of MetLife, Inc., New York, the largest life insurance company in the United States, with approximately $800 billion in total assets under management (AUM).

Beginning in 1996 and during his 11 years as Chief Investment Officer, he managed a diversified portfolio with total assets under management of approximately $2 billion. He provided leadership in setting up investment policies and strategies to enhance portfolio yield, implementation of asset allocation strategies to increase return on equity, and the oversight and implementation of risk management tools to achieve optimal return on capital.

Before joining MetLife, beginning in 1974 he was with JPMorgan Chase for 21 years in international banking and investment. He served as vice president in the areas of corporate lending, trade financing, institutional investment banking, and property-lending activities in New York and major Asian cities.

He has taught at the Graduate School of City University of New York (management science) and Beijing University (portfolio management).

During the past few years, he has been an active international conference speaker in Sydney, Hong Kong, Beijing, Seoul, Taipei, Bangkok, Kuala Lumpur, and Singapore on such global financial topics as portfolio management strategies, diversification and global investments, credit risk management, fixed-income investments and markets, and asset liability management, among others.

He received his undergraduate engineering degree from the University of Minnesota in Minneapolis and his MBA in Finance (cum laude) from St. Louis University, St. Louis, Missouri.

Since 2007, he has served as Adjunct Associate Professor of Finance at the University of Science and Technology in Hong Kong. In April 2012, he published a stock investment book in Hong Kong that was ranked a number-one bestseller on the popular Commercial Press Business Book Bestseller List.

Index